What readers a

After reading "The Pivota... ..... *μισισσεα this book in silence for quite some time. Story by story, I felt called to live more consciously, more empathetically and with a great deal more kindness. I suspect that you will as well.*
　—Dr. John Duffy, #1 Bestselling author of *The Available Parent*

A compelling, heartbreakingly personal read and a reminder that we need to take time to reflect on our choices and ask if the things we are good at, and bring us joy, can also make a difference in the world.
　— Carlene Ziegler, co-founder Artisan Partners Asset Management, philanthropist

After suffering an unimaginable tragedy, Jeff pursues a selfless, compassionate service to others, particularly the poorest and most vulnerable amongst us, and chronicles a powerful path for personal growth and fulfillment. A must-read for all ages.
　— George H. Hoff, Executive Vice President and Chief Financial Officer at Sargento Foods Inc.

We can't always choose what life throws at us, but we can choose our attitude towards it, believing that we have the power to create and re-create our lives, every day. We must live with intention, and create a life that takes our breath away. Jeff Wenzler is living proof. His book will compel you to look within and realize your purpose is to serve.
　— Nan Gardetto, Former owner and president of Gardetto Bakery and Baptista Bakery

Published by
HenschelHAUS Publishing, Inc.
www.henschelHAUSbooks.com

ISBN: 978159598-382-4 (paperback)
E-ISBN: 978159598-383-1 (Kindle)
E-ISBN: 978159598-384-8 (E-pub)

Publisher's Cataloging-In-Publication Data
(Prepared by The Donohue Group, Inc.)

Wenzler, Jeffrey.
The pivotal life : a compass for discovering purpose, passion & perspective / Jeffrey Wenzler.

pages : illustrations ; cm

Issued also in Kindle and ePub formats.
Publication date supplied by publisher.
ISBN: 978-1-59598-382-4 (paperback)

1. Wenzler, Jeffrey. 2. Self-actualization (Psychology) 3. Identity (Psychology) 4. Brothers and sisters--Death--Psychological aspects. 5. Conduct of life. I. Title.

BF637.S4 W46 2015 158.1   2015933926

Cover design by Dunn+Associates Design.
www.dunn-design.com

Photos by the author or used with permission.

Printed in the United States of America.

THE PIVOTAL LIFE

A COMPASS *for* DISCOVERING
PURPOSE, PASSION *&* PERSPECTIVE

JEFFREY WENZLER

Henschel
HAUS

MILWAUKEE, WISCONSIN

THE PIVOTAL LIFE

A COMPASS *for* DISCOVERING
PURPOSE, PASSION *&* PERSPECTIVE

Dedicated to my brother Joe

THE PIVOTAL LIFE COMPASS

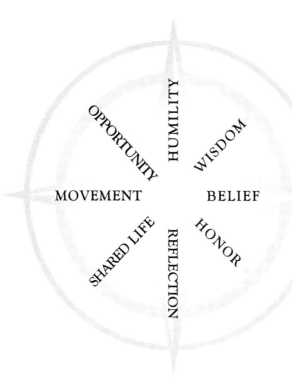

This book outlines life's compass,
each point a key component in living an extraordinary life.

TABLE OF CONTENTS

piv • ot • al

Of crucial importance in relation to the development
or success of something else.

FOREWORD

The day I first picked up *The Pivotal Life*, I was super busy. I had clients to call, a bunch of errands to run, a colleague I was desperately trying to get in touch with, and a workout I was perpetually putting on hold. I absently reached for Jeff's book. I wanted to check another item off my endless to-do list.

I was stopped immediately in my tracks. Jeff's stories drew me in, and I completed the read in one remarkable sitting. I sat and processed this book in silence for quite some time.

Jeff presents us here with a series of striking stories, drawn from his own life, ranging from the seemingly mundane at the surface, to the shocking; from the hilarious, to the tragic. As a reader, you will be along for quite a ride. And if you are like this reader, you will wonder why you have not been out there more: out of the familiar context, off the familiar continent, and forcing yourself into unfamiliar feelings and experiences. Story by story, you will find the payoff in Jeff's life has been priceless, and we will all benefit from the wealth of this brilliant, humble man's rich experience.

The stories in *The Pivotal Life* are strung together through a thread of inspiration, deep spirituality, and compassion for others and the Self. The message to me was abundantly clear. Slow down, take stock, and recognize those pivotal moments when they present themselves. I suspect you will be similarly inspired.

We all need to pause our lives and think about what we are doing, and why. Jeff's stories force you into emotional experience.

The Pivotal Life is a compelling read, and I am certain you will enjoy these important stories and messages. But more importantly, *The Pivotal Life* is a mandate for all of us. It calls each of us to live our lives more consciously, more empathically, and with a great deal more kindness than we may practice now.

Dr. John Duffy
#1 Bestselling author of *The Available Parent*

PREFACE

*Challenging the meaning of life is the truest expression
of the state of being human.*
—Viktor E. Frankl

A mother, exhausted from her seemingly never-ending work around the house, leaned over to pick up a notebook from the floor of her son's messy room. As she paged through it, she realized it was her son's Creative Writing journal. The lined pages were filled with random jottings, assignments, brainstorm lists, and incomplete stories that had been scratched down.

At the top of one page was a question her son had traced the letters over and over, as if in thought. It asked, "What is the pivotal life?"

Below the question was a laundry list of words and phrases her son had written:

Exceptional	*Adventurous*	*Extraordinary*
Meaningful	*Purposeful*	*Make a difference*
Unique	*Life-changing*	*Exciting*

Next, it read, "Complete this statement with one word."

The pivotal life is _____

Her son had written: "The pivotal life is meaningful."

The following day's assignment read, "Write your obituary." She read the following:

Kyle Thompson, of Green Bay, Wisconsin, born September 12, 1998, died last week peacefully in his sleep surrounded by his loved ones. Thompson died from complications arising from trauma sustained while rescuing a child from a collapsed building following an earthquake in Antigua, Guatemala. Thompson was on an extended service trip volunteering with the American Red Cross. Thompson was known as a tireless and dedicated humanitarian and died the way he lived— serving others. The little girl he saved will be giving his eulogy this Friday with the help of the Governor of the State of Wisconsin. A memorial fund to open a school dedicated in his honor has been established. Kyle's last wishes were to have inscribed on his gravestone: "He lived a pivotal life."

The mother stared at the thought-filled words in her son's spiral notebook. She had worked hard to provide her children a good life. They had a nice home in a safe neighborhood, financial security, a strong school system, a welcoming church community, loving parents, and great friendships.

So what was it that drew her son's heart elsewhere? Why was he so attracted by lands struggling with poverty and tragedy? None of what she considered a "full" life were included in his definition of a "pivotal" life. But she seemed to understand. A deep sense of pride rushed through her.

That day, in her quiet home, the apprentice had taught the master. The mother's eyes—and heart—were opened. Placing the laundry basket on the floor, the mother sat at the kitchen table, ignoring the sink filled with breakfast dishes, the pile of bills to be paid lying before her on the table, and asked herself, "What is a pivotal life?"

Kyle was not looking for a nice life, a safe life, or even a great life. He craved a meaningful life, and so did she.

* * * * *

No matter where we are on our lifelines, we often find ourselves contemplating why we are doing what we are doing, and what our greater purpose is. We are voyeurs who watch with admiration as others live with purpose. We revere people living passionately, and only when we take a break to think about life and our place in it, do we ask ourselves how we can live a pivotal life as well.

The Pivotal Life is a life of meaningful purpose, lived with exhilarating passion and insightful perspective. But how do we get there? Is a pivotal life a destination—or a way of life?

The aim of this book is to share lessons learned from my own pivotal moments presented to me by life. I am an ordinary person who lives an extraordinary life. It is not without heartache and struggle, certainly, but the purpose that shapes my confidence, and the passion that soars through my veins, has given me perspective about the world in which I live that is surely worth being called—pivotal.

Life is a mosaic of experiences and relationships that beckon a response from your heart. It is these heartfelt and heart-stopping moments that influence your mind and then motivate your actions. The Pivotal Life is an internal backpack that contains a compass calibrated by its past to navigate the future.

Living *The Pivotal Life* is a mindset. Along my own journey, I have discovered eight points by which to calibrate the compass of life. This compass guides my mind, my body, and my spirit.

As you accompany me through these pages, you will laugh with me, struggle with me, rejoice with me, cry with me, and grow with me. This book, *The Pivotal Life*, is for you.

Allow me to be your guide using the compass of life. I promise to be honest and sincere. My hope is that when you have finished this short shared journey, that you will look at your own place in the world with new eyes and in a different light. It is also my wish that you might be better equipped to change the world—by changing you!

If some of the words do not make you feel a bit uncomfortable or some of the concepts don't challenge you, then I have not done my job in showing you a way to live a more authentic, pivotal life. Living a pivotal life does not always come easy. There is no growth in the arena of comfort, and no comfort in the arena of growth. The arena of growth is a path of discovery leading away from a life of mediocrity.

You will be introduced to eight pivotal points of the compass that can lead you to an extraordinary landscape. The characters within this book, witnessed through my eyes, are common people and events that unintentionally provide perspective on who we are and who we can become.

The eight points used to calibrate our internal compass of life are:

1) *Humility*
2) *Wisdom*
3) *Belief*
4) *Honor*
5) *Reflection*
6) *Shared Life*
7) *Movement*
8) *Opportunity*

I believe these are the key components to living *a pivotal life*. They will empower you to travel outside the ordinary and into the land of the extraordinary. Surely, you will also add your own points to that internal compass.

The *pivotal life* is waiting for you. In fact, it is all around you!

Enjoy the journey!
Jeff Wenzler

.

THE THRESHOLD

Joe and Jeff Wenzler as kids

My brother Joe, age 21

Breathless

*Sometimes it is the same moments that take your breath away
that breathe purpose and love back into your life.*
—Steve Maraboli

"No, Jeff, I am the first to go!" were the last words my 25-year-old brother spoke here on earth. Five minutes later, he collapsed into my arms and died.

One moment, I was amidst the security of my family, hanging out with my big brother on my twentieth birthday, and the next instant, all that I had taken for granted my entire life was tossed into my face. I was thrown into a whirlwind that no one is ever prepared for at such a young age—in fact, at any age.

It had all begun a few weeks before when I declined to go to a family wedding in Minnesota. I had just transferred colleges and had been taken under the wings of a great group of friends who wanted to take me out for my birthday the same weekend as the wedding. The last thing I wanted to do for my twentieth birthday was to spend it driving five hours from Milwaukee to Minneapolis, only to hear, "Oh, how you've grown into a young man … " and be asked about school. Plans were made and I was going to stay in Milwaukee and enjoy a sense of independence from a family function.

Days before the wedding, my older sister had called from Utah with the intent of changing my decision about attending. My mind was made up, but I listened anyway, out of respect. Her sisterly wisdom caused me to pivot and agree to join the family. My one condition was that I could drive with my big brother, Joe.

The five-hour journey was a trip back in time. Joe and I laughed about family, girls, and life. We were two brothers enjoying the freedom of the open road. I hadn't felt that good about our relationship in years. Joe was older, had a job, was married, and ducked out of most family functions. On occasion, I had wondered if we would ever recapture our brotherly bond from childhood.

Throughout high school, baseball was my passion and I was quite a good pitcher. I would search the stands from the pitching mound looking for my brother, hoping he would see me play. Yet, he never showed.

Sitting in my brother's car, riding shotgun, listening to music, and shooting the breeze, made all those missed years disappear.

When we arrived at the hotel where my extended family was staying, I went inside to say hello. Joe stayed behind—surprise, surprise. As I gave my sister a big hug to thank her for convincing me to come, my cousin Danny approached us. He was the one getting married the next day.

Danny knew Joe well from living together for a summer and was interested in how he was doing. He knew that Joe had battled partying and drugs for years. Joe had been out of a rehabilitation clinic for four years. As far as anyone knew, his drug habits were old news.

Danny asked how he was doing with the "stuff." My sister, as taken aback from the question as I at the time, hesitantly said, "Yeah… he's doing ok."

Then Danny said, "You know that 'stuff,'" as he mimicked a sniff, "is hard to get away from. It'll kill ya."

There wasn't much more to that conversation, but it was a foreshadowing of the coming day.

The next morning, the family assembled for breakfast, and made plans to blow some time before the wedding at the well-known, enormous Mall of America. I was wished a happy birthday from all and we set off to shop. The pilgrimage to the mall included myself, my mother, my sister and her future husband, my aunt, my uncle and my godson, my brother, his wife, and his step-daughter. My father stayed back at the hotel to study for a class he was taking.

When we arrived at the mall, I was told that I could pick out my birthday present. My brother and I were drawn to a gigantic sporting goods store. The place had everything. I was sure to find a gift in that athlete's paradise.

The previous year, I had a coming of age experience—in a brotherly sense—and had been invited to play on Joe's bar league softball team. I was trying out all the softball bats in the store and asked Joe to help me select the perfect one. My ego felt our 1-12 record of wins was due to the bats instead of those swinging them.

However, Joe's fascination was on something else. His eyes were fixated on an interactive golf simulator. Childlike excitement flooded through us and we both darted for the door. However, just before getting to the cage door, Joe put his best basketball move on me, boxing me out with his long arms and pointy elbows. As far back as I could remember, my big brother had put me in my place—especially in sports. Joe was very tall—six foot six, to be exact. I had finally caught up to him in height, but he was still more naturally athletic than I was.

Just before we entered, Joe looked at me and said, "No, Jeff, I'm the first to go." Then he strode through the golf simulator's caged door.

Joe had picked out a new golf club from the rack and teed up in front of the simulator's screen. I laughed as he hacked a few balls off center into the computerized screen. Watching Joe golf reminded me of a summer day on the public golf course with him and a cold six-pack.

When Joe finished his swings, I eagerly went to the cart to pick my own club. I began asking him which to use. As I turned to him, I saw that look. Oh God, that look! His hands were on his knees, head down, bent at the waist.

"Aw, man, I feel like I'm gonna faint." He reached out his hand toward the cart that held the clubs where I was standing. His hand clutched the cart and my hand as he searched for balance. There was no balance to be found.

As if moving in slow motion, as it still is in my mind to this day, his strength melted and he fell over, taking the cart of clubs and me with him to the floor. Golf clubs scattered all around us. He immediately went into convulsions, his body thrusting out every last bit of energy. I could only sit there, holding him, baffled and scared as to why his body was reacting in such a grotesque manner.

Time didn't exist, only the reality of my brother's failing body slipping through my grasp. I recall staring in utter confusion, not knowing what to do, and a deep sense of helplessness. Somewhere along the line, I looked through the wired cage of the simulator into the crowd of stunned onlookers, seeing a few scattered, familiar faces. I saw their first expressions: confusion, realization... terror.

Next thing I knew, a man was kneeling on the other side of my sprawled-out, seizuring brother. He said he was a doctor. He was calm and collected, the opposite of me. He was caressing my brother, while trying to ease my worry and panic. Perhaps he knew something I did not about this unraveling nightmare. After all, he was the doctor. Perhaps he was too calm.

Why is he doing this? Shouldn't he be doing something? I wondered.

In the computerized golf game my brother had been playing, you couldn't lose a ball no matter how much you shanked it.

It looked as though a life could be lost if something wasn't done. This wasn't a simulator you could restart anytime you like. It was my brother's life, fading away right before my eyes, like a golf ball sailing away into the distance.

Finally, I murmured, "Something's not right. Something's gotta be done." My brother had been writhing on the floor with a seizure, and I assumed, since Joe was so young, the doctor thought he was just having a grand mal seizure and it would eventually pass.

I'll never know if it was the terrible tone of my voice or if the doctor simply realized the same god-awful thing I had been watching from the start. My brother's face had gone from a clammy white to a deep purple. Maybe the doctor was more concerned for the welfare of my brother's body as it thrashed around in an inhuman manner. Perhaps he couldn't see Joe's face. Joe's face, which was so familiar to me.

I had been instructed to hold Joe's head back to help keep his airway clear. I was right there, filled with dread. My brother had stopped convulsing. The timeless silence that had brought a deeper and deeper color to Joe's face needed to be broken.

The doctor, in no more than the time it would take for my dreadful observation to register, finally said something that shattered the silence. In a non-reassuring voice, he called out, "What is going on here?" This crumpled any hope that was struggling to find its way through the mass confusion. The doctor suddenly went from calm and collected to frantic, as he pushed me out of the way to search for a non-existent pulse before administering CPR.

I felt even more naked and vulnerable, not being able to hold on to my brother. I was in a cage of all things, being gawked at by strangers watching the CPR ... helpless. Was this hell on earth?

At least it seems like Joe is breathing, my mind told me. But no, it wasn't his breath. It was only air and saliva being repulsed from a body that had given up and no longer could make use of the doctor's gift of life.

"Where are the paramedics? Somebody call the damned paramedics!" I could hear this among many muffled voices.

Were those words coming from my mind, my family, the crowd of strangers, or from my own mouth?

"Where are the goddamned paramedics?" I finally heard myself scream again.

An audience had arrived but there was no music. I was just sitting there in the spotlight on the stage of life, doing nothing while people watched. Time was at a standstill.

Will I make it to the end of the show? Where are the paramedics? Will somebody please get help? My brother is dying, my heart shouted.

By that time, many members of my family had arrived and stood clutching one another. How can everything be so secure one moment and the next so chaotic? How can you have everything and then watch it slip away as if it had never existed? Those same questions were reflected in the not-yet-teary eyes of my family. Their expressions portrayed the same confusion and shock I felt throbbing throughout my own body, that prevented me from standing up.

The only thing I knew for sure was that I would not leave my brother's side until he had been brought back from where I feared he had gone.

Moments later, my family had entered my worst nightmare as they began filing into the cage. They were no longer outsiders looking in. The cage was a symbolic stage that had a far different perspective from my vantage point.

My family was the cast of the play, and the drama was unfolding in front of the strangers who stood outside.

My mother appeared and fell to her knees, shouting at her elder son to pull through. At a loss for rational words, she then took on Satan by yelling at him to stay away from her child. It was as if Joe's repulsed breaths from the CPR were responses to her plea for mercy. More doctors and EMTs gathered around, offering assistance.

The off-duty angels in civilian clothes in the form of doctors from the crowded mall had all woken up in a similar manner as my family that brisk October morning. They had the same intention of tackling the monstrous Mall of America, yet instead, they were now trying to buy an unusual gift ... the life of a young man. A frantic, crying mother berating Satan had likely never been part of their first responder training.

I wanted so dearly to pull my mother away and comfort her. I wanted to tell her, as she had told me so often in my life, that everything would be OK. But I didn't. I couldn't. I felt she was doing just as much good for my brother as the people who were hopelessly blowing air into his lungs. The fading color in his face and periodic voices exclaiming, "Still no pulse" confirmed that fact.

Was there nothing to grab hold of as a point of reference to get me back to shore? Prayer was all that was left for us, so I joined my mom. Side by side, we prayed for the life of the big brother I had looked up to for 20 years, a life to which my mother had given birth. We prayed and prayed.

The paramedics had taken over as the helpful, but exhausted, off-duty doctors and trained citizens blended back into the crowd. The paramedics were scurrying around, each doing his or her own task. "What was going on? Why had someone so young had a massive heart attack?"

Somehow my legs brought me to an upright position for the first time since they had carried me into the confines of the caged-in, astro-turfed space.

My brother's wife was standing on the other side of the simulator's cage door. Her presence was the only thing that prevented my rage from escaping. I was a caged animal furious for being in the situation I found myself. I wanted answers.

My brother did drugs, but to what extent I didn't know—or was it that I did not want to know? The fact is, though, he did. I was on autopilot. I grabbed the wires of the cage and yelled, "Karin, what is he on?"

She was as stunned as I was with the words that came from her lips in a whisper, "He smoked crack cocaine."

I don't remember my reaction. I had no response.

I turned and began telling the large group of paramedics that the big brother I had looked up to was sprawled out on the floor dead because he had smoked crack cocaine. Anyone gathered around the spectacle could hear the humiliating fact.

The onlookers and medical personnel were complete strangers. Joe's use of crack cocaine was a dark secret, and it was my birthday. I would never be the same. I had gone from being an innocent teenager straight into the harsh, nightmare realities of adulthood in a matter of one stunning statement.: "He smoked crack cocaine."

I returned to my mother's side, kneeling down and holding her and Joe, praying. We were forced to release our grasp as electricity was zapped into the lifeless body of my 25-year-old brother. It was a futile attempt to bring back my brother from a place where only prayer could now help.

Procedurally, oxygen and injections of one sort or another were stuffed into my brother until he could be transported to the nearest hospital. By no means was I upset that so many people were trying so hard to revive his life. Somehow I knew too much time had passed with no sign of recovery.

In my mind, I knew he had died in my arms not long after he initially collapsed. That is when his heart stopped beating on its own. I didn't want to fully admit his death, so I continued to pray and hold onto his arm as the gurney transported Joe's limp form through the crowds, the mall, and parking lot, until I had to let go for the ambulance to take him away.

I'm glad I didn't have to see myself holding on to my brother as he was wheeled through the mall. I never took my eyes off of him. The gurney guided my direction. It was as though I were in a trance. It must have looked so pathetic and sad seeing the expressions of shock on my family's faces as they all followed my brother's corpse through a mall like it was some kind of parade of mourners.

Before Joe was lifted into the ambulance, I remember the paramedics trying to fit his legs into the parking structure elevator and thinking how he was bigger than life. This thought lasted only a moment, for I saw my mother standing alone in the desolate parking lot.

Since my dad was the only family member who had not come to the mall, I went straight to her, the stand-in man of the family. We were both escorted in a police car behind the ambulance to the hospital, where we would meet up with the rest of the family and the fate of our loved one. As we followed the ambulance, my mother and I silently came to an initial point of closure. We knew it looked grim and that our worst nightmare was being fulfilled.

My first tears welled as my mom clung to me and confided what she always silently prayed. She still had hope, but she was preparing herself. Her words had a harshness to them, but it was turning out to be a harsh world. She said she had always prayed that if Joe was not cleaned out and healed of his addiction on earth, that she would rather have him be at peace and clean with God.

Time seemed to stand still. I knew the final proclamation was awaiting us at the approaching hospital.

Only twenty minutes had passed since Joe collapsed. Hell's clock is quite slow.

At the hospital, my family was given one of those private rooms outside the emergency room. The room was furnished with everything from Kleenex to a chaplain. I had no desire to wait in a claustrophobic room full of tears for the doctor to return with an update. How many times would he leave and return before bringing us the painful, inevitable words? It was like playing Russian Roulette. Sooner or later, he would bring with him the bullet that would pierce our hearts.

Joe was dead. I knew it, but did I want to admit it or lose it in front of my whole family? I wanted so desperately to remain strong for my mom. The room was too goddamned small, and getting smaller every time a tear was added to it.

I struggled to keep it together and be there for my family. Our bonds were being tested. Everything from the enclosing walls to the enveloping hugs, squeezed out what remaining patience and control I had.

Anger welled up in my chest, which hope had vacated. *Why had my brother put his family in this situation? Why me? It was my birthday.*

The idea of my father arriving to all of this didn't help any. The thought of the phone call he received back at the hotel made me shudder inside. I wondered if time would stand still, just as still as it had for me, while he fought traffic on the way to the hospital. Can you imagine enduring the wait at a stoplight, knowing that your son's life was in limbo? How had my dad felt, knowing that everyone most important in his son's life was with him when this all happened—except for him, his father?

The waiting was tearing me up inside. I needed to hit something or break something. My emotions intensified with the passing of each timeless minute. All I could find within reach in that unbearable instant were a couple of pamphlets on a reading table next to me. *When in Need of*

Prayer. I saw that right before I began venting my anger on the pamphlet. The last thing I needed at that moment was to sit down and read how to approach this situation. Nature was taking its own natural course.

As I began ripping and squeezing the inanimate life out of the pamphlet, a tiny word in the middle of the page caught my eye. It was my brother's name, Joseph. I stopped ripping immediately and began to read his name in its context. It was an Old Testament scripture passage, along with words from some psychologist on the topic of death. It read, "...but Joseph said to them, do not be afraid! Am I in the place of God?"

I cannot adequately explain what happened at that moment in human terms, but it was a transformation, an understanding, and an acceptance. All I knew for sure was that amidst all the pain, anguish, and confusion, I understood. I understood with all my mind, heart, and soul. I understood like I understood that night precedes day. In that moment, I didn't know what to do with this realization except to know deep down that it was some kind of spiritual gift.

Without putting any thought into it, I immediately knew that my brother was with God. It wasn't that I hoped he was, or made myself believe he was. Rather, I knew he was. I had seen him die before my eyes as I held his body in my arms. Right then, I knew he was not only gone from our physical lives, but had entered the next world, and he was okay. Joe was no longer missing. His place had been established and I could feel it soar through my soul. I didn't know why the gift of acceptance and understanding was given to me, but I did know that I would have a lifetime to make sense out of it.

This revelation made such an impact on me that I didn't even wait for my father to arrive, or the priest, or the doctor, to pronounce my brother "officially" deceased. I left. My family still had hope, but for some reason, I knew the hope was gone and that Joe was now in God's arms.

All this happened within an hour of my last conversation with Joe. Time is strange.

I walked out of the hospital and continued walking off the hospital grounds until I came upon a grassy hill where I sat down and leaned against a bare tree. I looked all around me at the colorful autumn leaves that also had lived such short lives. The sun was shining down on me as I looked up, although the incredible feeling was from within.

I found myself smiling, while saying, "Thank you." It was like passing off a loved one into the care of a loving friend. A seed of acceptance was born. Nothing else in the world mattered at that moment. It would still be a tough, lonely time, but life had changed, and so had my path. This was my pivotal moment.

REFLECTION QUESTIONS

- Have you ever experienced a "breathless" moment?
- How did it cause you to look at your life differently?
- What questions arose from this event?
- How did you grow from this event?

NOTES

SOLITUDE

It's your road, and yours alone.
Others may walk it with you, but no one can walk it for you.
—Rumi

The compass of life is often the result of pivotal moments. When a wave strikes and throws us off balance, even leaves us breathless, we search for perspective. Living the pivotal life is the pursuit of discovering a guiding force that will allow us to view our human experience and grow from it—but sometimes the adversity we face hurts like hell.

With regard to my experience, when I decided to return to the hospital, my father had arrived and everything intensified. Even though I knew my brother had passed and was now at peace, we, as a family, were not. I was still very vulnerable to the human emotions. My father's reaction to Joe's condition set off emotions within that couldn't be controlled.

After I was able to dry my tears, the chaplain returned, carrying with him the inevitable news of my brother's death. My family was allowed to visit Joe for a final time, but I declined. I had seen enough that day and had the whole tragedy sorted out as well as could be expected. I felt that by seeing Joe in such lifeless silence would ruin anything I had achieved, or had been gifted. I would have to start looking out for my best interests if I was to ever make sense out of what was happening to me.

Although I was far from thinking logically at the time, I was open to what was occurring… open as a wound is open, but nonetheless, open. In retrospect, that may have been the key to my healing. I was vulnerable and hurt, but I was willing to accept the changes in my life. The *Serenity Prayer* sums it up appropriately: "God grant me the serenity to accept the things I cannot change, the courage to change the things I can, and the wisdom to know the difference."

After an hour, my brother's wife still hadn't returned from the emergency room, so I went to help pull her away from her lost love. As I entered the ER, the lifeless silence was even worse than I had imagined. The only thing breaking that silence was Karin's conversation with her departed husband. She sat at his side, caressing his hair amidst the million-dollar medical technology that could not bring him back from where his recreational drug habits had taken him. Drugs had beaten the countless hours of medical training of all the angels in the flesh who had tirelessly attempted to revive my brother. The sight was too much, and the one-sided conversation between wife and husband, too personal. I will never forget that image.

I knew my brother was gone and I knew he was in a better place, but that did not prevent all the questions, regrets, anger, and pain, from arising out of the silence of death. I let my sister-in-law's conversation go on as long as I could bear. Before escorting Karin from the room, I walked over to Joe's body, grabbed a pair of surgical scissors that was lying on a counter, and cut off a piece of his sweatshirt.

As a youngster and teen, I always wanted to be like my big brother. I would often borrow his clothes, even if they were too big for me. I'd always have to give them back, but this would be one sweatshirt I would never wear. Cutting away a 3-inch square of the light gray fabric with trembling fingers was like taking Joe with me.

To this day, the piece of cloth brings to mind the birthday present I never received, and serves as a reminder to me that all actions in life have consequences. The love I left behind in the emergency room that day pivoted me drastically in a new direction.

A REBIRTH

I experienced all forms of Joe's death, including his rebirth into another life, as well as a rebirth of my own. I didn't know it at the time, but as I sit here today, years later, I am still amazed how a pivotal moment can influence one's life.

On the way back to Milwaukee along the same road I had driven so joyfully and carefree the day before with my brother, I could only stare out the window into the transforming autumn colors of the Northwoods. I thought of a song I once heard, "...seasons change, feelings change, people change." How right it was. Had the unknown songwriter in my mind experienced something similar? Had anyone? How alone would I be with this tragedy? How would the life I left behind a day earlier, at home and college, react to such an event? Those were some of the thoughts I recall as the sun began to set on that first day. Would it ever be as beautiful again?

When our caravan of five households finally finished our road trip back from hell, my mom told me what my brother's 12-year-old step-daughter had said about his death. "Joe loved everyone so much his heart couldn't take it, so it just broke." Oh, how a child's innocence can simplify such a tragedy. Maybe there is something to seeing life through the eyes of a child.

Before I attempted sleeping that first night at my parents' home, I busied myself with unpacking the suitcase I had never even gotten the chance to open. As I pulled out the clothes I was supposed to be wearing right then at the wedding, I could only think about how this tragic turn of events had affected my relatives. What's worse—a loved one dying on your birthday or on your wedding day?

As I pulled the last piece of clothing from my bag, a present and card dropped onto the floor. The girl I had been dating at school had secretly placed a gift in my bag for me to find on my birthday. Bad timing. I slowly opened the card and it read, "I hope you have a wonderful birthday and a lot of fun. Wish I was with you!" I cried... and not from joy.

That night, the Wenzler household was silent in the darkness, yet no one was able to sleep much. As for me, I couldn't stop replaying my brother's last words, last look, his collapse, and last expelled breath. It had all happened so suddenly, but my mind had recorded every last detail, etched into my being. Those moments replayed in my mind for a week straight.

Just like the aftershocks of an earthquake can be stronger than the original quake, so too are the emotions after a death. Waking up at my childhood home that next morning was rough. Something was different. I felt partly well rested and secure in my own bed, but something wasn't right. Why was I in my own bed when I lived at school? It took but a split second to realize that it had not been a nightmare. That second was long enough to relive the entire death of my brother. It is amazing how the human mind can operate. It was the day after World War III and I would have to go downstairs and encounter the aftermath.

I decided to postpone the inevitable as long as possible. My father had told the family the night before that we were going to Sunday morning mass as usual and no one was about to argue. I took my time getting ready for church and for some reason, I grasped a Bible stashed away on a dusty shelf. I was amazed by what I found.

The first page I opened to was Psalm 6. It read, "Be merciful to me, Lord, for I am faint." *Faint* had been the last word my brother uttered before he collapsed and died in my arms. "*Aw, man, I feel like I'm going to faint.*"

My Faith

To explain how these types of strange coincidences affected me, I must first set the stage for you on who I was before this all occurred. I came from a Catholic family and considered myself a Christian, but I never really knew the depth of my faith. Sure, I went to church, but the length of the service was about as long as my Christian identity lasted. I wasn't a bad person necessarily; rather, I just went about my teenage life doing as I pleased day by day.

The last thing I would have done, at that point in my life, was to turn to the Bible to seek advice or learn how to survive high school or college life. In fact, if I had not gone to the wedding that weekend, I probably would have taken my girlfriend and other friends back to my parents' house for one hell of a birthday party. Imagine my family returning late that Saturday night to a kitchen full of college buddies playing beer pong.

I took my stunned look and discovery of the Bible passage down the hall to my parents' room, where I showed my mom what I had just read. The look on her face was as stunned as mine, but for a different reason. She had been given the exact same Psalm when my brother was in drug rehab years earlier. Like so many mothers with addicted children, she wondered where she had gone wrong raising her child, and turned over every last bit of her strength and anxiety to her God.

The part of Psalm 6 that touched her so and that she had held close to her heart for so many years, were verses 6 through 9: "I am worn out from my groaning. All night long I flood my bed with weeping and drench my couch with tears. My eyes grow weak with sorrow; they fail because of all my foes. Away from me, all you who do evil, for the Lord has heard my weeping. The Lord has heard my cry for mercy; the Lord accepts my prayer."

My mother was sick of crying herself to sleep at night and watching my family being torn apart at the seams, which she spent a lifetime stitching out of love. She knew her Lord was there for her.

And here He was for me, dropping another reminder that all was going to be okay. Grief is like working out. You know it all will be better eventually, but for the moment, it hurts like hell and it's bound to get worse before it gets better. All I could do is store the short, yet powerful, message from above, in my heart to fill the crack I felt widening inside. The grace of God was working slowly, but I just had a chunk of my life ripped from me.

I had been stung, cheated, stripped naked in front of a strange crowd, and robbed by the rabid clutches of tragic death. I was left spinning inside, falling in darkness, searching for direction, searching for answers. Each minute that passed brought new questions. Oh, so many questions. Would I ever find the answers? Would I make it through all this?

During church service that morning, I thought to myself that I would never find meaning in what had happened. As I looked around at all the people in the congregation, I remember thinking that I was on my own with this search for meaning. It would be a solo journey. They didn't know what had happened, they weren't there, and they would never understand my hell. I wanted to scream out and tell them and try to make them relate, but I couldn't.

The reality of loss was upon me like a blood rush from standing too quickly, preventing clarity. My equilibrium was damaged and instead of giving in and collapsing, I stumbled forward, unclear, deeper into the fog. I wanted to stop and not move until things were clear. But I couldn't. The fast-moving freeway of life was already moving. It wouldn't make any exceptions for me. Why was it that the world couldn't understand that I needed to stop and figure out what was happening to me? I had questions with few answers.

Get moving or be dragged—that was my new reality. I felt this as my father drove me back to my college campus, about 30 minutes away, to pick up my things so I could temporarily move home. I was glad to be living close to my family who had endured the same nightmare the previous day, but my friends on campus had no clue. I would be naked yet again, burning in the sun, pleading for shelter.

As we journeyed down the freeway, I clenched my teeth and looked back toward home, wishing I could return.

> *Only days earlier, I had been a boy on a footpath, but now, I was a man climbing an unforgiving mountain. I was different. Life was now different. My outlook would have to be different.*

The ride in the car with my father reminded me of an experience I had as a child. There was this time when my sixth grade teacher was so upset with my behavior in class that she called home to speak with my parents. Those dreaded calls home as a child meant multiple lectures on respect, maturity, and facing up to one's actions. My father demanded all three. It was one thing to break down and promise change and apologize to my folks, yet quite another to have to succumb to the tyranny of the sixth-grade, ornery, pregnant, math teacher.

My father told me I would have to apologize. I refused to swallow my pride and obey his wishes. I yelled immaturely, "No way, you're crazy!" Big mistake. Huge mistake. My father was an executive who was not used to taking orders from a cracked-voice, pubescent, know-it-all. His response was to the point, "Not only are you going to apologize, young man, but I am going to take you personally to school first thing in the morning and make sure you do!" No threats, no force, no compromise. It was a simple statement from a man who expected nothing less. I'll never forget the anxiety of that car ride.

Once again, I found myself in the car with my father heading away from home toward school to face a fire. I had gone through worse in the past 24 hours, but I was weakening from the blows of loss. I wanted to be at home. I wanted four walls surrounding me and one door that would open and close at my command.

The exit was approaching: Marquette University ... one mile ... half a mile ... a quarter mile. I clenched my jaw to its breaking point as I privately pleaded for the car to continue past the exit. It was as if the tightening of my jaw played a mechanical role in the deceleration of the car as it veered onto the exit. It was that sickening feeling you get on a roller coaster, which at one point was bearable, yet the approaching twists and turns become anything but wel-comed. My stomach was left somewhere behind the car.

Two blocks later, we pulled up slowly in front of the doors to my dorm. As the car came to a hesitant halt, my father's eyes met mine as I looked up eight floors to my dorm room window. I could feel his compassion as he asked if I wanted him to come with me. It was almost a rhetorical question. We both knew I would have to do this on my own. It was not a question of simply gathering up my things to move back home with my tail between my legs. It was much more. It was a challenge, a battle.

I was a competitive guy who rarely asked for help. I felt beaten down and to me, that was an exposed weakness. Looking back, I realize that there are no points given to a person for hiding his pain. In fact, possessing the humility to express emotion is a strength. Notice, I said "looking back."

At the time, I did everything I could to keep my emotions at bay. I wondered if I could make it through that massive corridor, elevator, and hallway filled with people?

They were not just people, though. They were the people I lived with. I had only transferred to Marquette a month and a half earlier. The guys on my floor were still getting to know me and now I didn't even feel as if I knew myself. They now represented granules of salt and I was the exposed wound. Thoughts raced through my mind saying, "Steer clear of anyone you know and avoid any additional pain."

I felt as if my pain was obvious. I might as well have been wearing a sandwich board on my body that announced my distress and despair. I was one of those reversible jackets; only the side I was showing was a side never worn before in public. I was walking into a building containing more than 500 of my peers. I felt exposed. I thought they all knew. Or was it worse that I may have to explain to someone what had happened? Oh, God!

Up to that point, someone else had acted as a cushion, protecting me, telling others what had happened. People were somewhat prepared and those who were not comfortable around tragedy could bow out from talking to me in an attempt not to make the situation any worse than it already was. For years after Joe's death, people who had known both of us seemed to walk on thin ice, not knowing exactly what to say.

The first moments around friends who hadn't heard about Joe were awkward. As an example, when over a year had passed after Joe's death, a distant relative met up with me only minutes before the start of my sister's wedding. When she was introduced, because it had been so many years since we had seen one another, she said, "Oh, you're the boy in whose arms Joey died." Need I search for another more perfect example of the awkwardness that surrounds death?

Like so many things in life, the anxiety leading up to an event is usually worse than the actual experience. This was true as far as my journey through the dorm was concerned. Life continued on even though my brother's did not. I slowly realized it was me that was making this experience worse then it needed to be. My mind was playing tricks on my senses. I knew it, but had no energy, or will, to do anything about it.

I was in shock. My awareness was so acute I could pick up random conversations of people I did not even know just to see if they were talking about me. The hallway leading to my room seemed to stretch like Silly Putty, like the infamous hallway in the movie, *The Shining*. The farther I traveled, the farther away to room seemed to me.

When I finally reached the poster-covered destination I had called home for the past month and a half, I slowly opened the door, hoping that I would only find a mess with no carbon-based life forms. My luck seemed to have taken an abrupt turn for the worse. Behind my heavy dorm room door, I found some friends watching football. After all, it was Packer Sunday. They were watching the game Joe and I had made a bet on and planned on seeing together only days before. I can now, only years later, say that Joe was offered better seats and ended up watching it with Vince Lombardi.

The guys said, "Hi" and I murmured something in response as I sat on the floor pretending to watch the game. The football players began to blur as I fought back tears. Someone asked me how my weekend was, and from that moment on, I only remember a few thoughts. I remember not looking anyone straight in the eye. I remember talking while staring at the TV screen. I remember willing myself to breathe, and I remember completely turning over the mood in the entire dorm once I spoke.

THE SOLO JOURNEY

Although I didn't know it at that time, as spiritual as the journey may be to healing and understanding, it must be taken alone. There is a great deal of solitude in tragedy and healing. Sure, there are people that help you along the way, but only you can make the journey. It is up to you, and only you, to open yourself up and start the journey toward recovery. It sounds lonely, and it is.

Some may disagree with this, but I have found that no matter how many hugs or charitable advice I received, that everything would be all right in time, a void was still left behind. I had to work from the inside out, not the other way around. I had to face my inner feelings in order to survive in the outside world.

The Pivotal Life is a life of circumstance. Simply put, life is constantly moving, shifting, and evolving. Life is a wave with beauty and turmoil. It can catapult you to new heights and pull you down within a gasp. My pivotal moment in life losing my brother set me on a wild ride in search of meaning. The following poem, by a mother who found perspective in life's struggle, might help someone who also questions the meaning in life's tumultuous waves.

The Waves of Life
By Sara Rosenfeld

Ride the waves of life my friend
Some high, some fierce, some with no end
But you'll not be washed away by them
If you can ride the waves of life my friend

Weights may try to pull you down
Emotions full of pain
But hold on to a board
And ride the waves my friend

A board will keep you up above
The water deep and mean
And let you ride the waves of life
Ride the waves with ease

And what's the board, this heaven sent
To hold on to in the sea?
This board my friend is nothing new
You had it all along with you
But you have to know it's there before
You can use its strength to hold and more
The board my friend, is nothing new
It's just the strength of the inner you

So ride the waves of life my friend
Ride the waves with ease
Let the water splash your face
Like grass sprinkled with dew
For you can still keep the pace
IF you hold on to the strength of the real you

And ride the waves of life

REFLECTION QUESTIONS

- Can you name a time when you felt you had to deal with something alone?

- Oftentimes, pivotal moments are struggles or challenges. What things enabled you to sustain the struggle and hopefully get through it?

- If you have not yet encountered a pivotal moment in your life, how has someone you know handled one of life's waves?

NOTES

HUMILITY

My brother's grave

The Leap of Faith

*The best way to find yourself
is to lose yourself in the service of others.*
—Mahatma Gandhi

After burying my brother, I found myself sitting under yet another small tree on a cold autumn day, seeking perspective—or perhaps enlightenment—this time at the cemetery. I stared at Joe's new gravestone. There were his birth date and his death date (the same as my own birthday). I began reflecting. The first thought was a multi-faceted question just starting to grow in my mind, "Was Joe's death on my birthday a sort of gift? Was it a chance for a re-birth? Was there meaning within it?"

Next, I became hyper-focused on the space between those two dates. The space represented all the days of his life. Instead of beating myself up with all the couldas, wouldas, and shouldas of Joe's difficult life, I thought about my own space. In the big picture, our own spaces are but moments in time. However, our short time on earth is filled with great opportunity. At my age of twenty, roughly one fourth of my life, if it too were not cut short, was already gone. I wanted my space to represent making a difference. To do this, I first had to discover my purpose. This would take a leap of faith.

To take that leap, I had to act courageously, if it meant stepping out of my comfort zone. Within three months of Joe's passing, I was standing in line at the airport with two enormous rucksacks bulging with donated toothbrushes and deflated soccer balls, headed for Guatemala City in Central America.

A friend of the family had connected me with a mission outpost where I could volunteer with the poor. I didn't ask many questions. I just needed to get out of town and start searching for meaning in life. Why not in a Third World country, one in the throes of civil war, and whose language I couldn't speak?

Due to some tropical depression, my flight was re-routed and eventually canceled. I showed up a day late in Guatemala City, but my suitcase with clothes did not. I had no ride to pick me up, no clothes, and *"no hablo espanol."*

Sitting in Spanish class in high school is far different than *absorbing* Spanish. You cannot learn a language through osmosis. I had sat in the back row of class, cocky as hell, wondering why the heck I needed to learn a foreign language. Instead of taking a Spanish nickname like "Juan," I gave myself the name, "Taco." "Nacho" and "Burrito" sat to my left and "Dorito" sat to my right. They cared about learning the language as much as I did.

The only thing I learned was how to make *"Torte de Chocolate con ExLax."* You read that right! My *amigos* in class and I had to bake a treat for the end-of-year Mexican Fiesta. It was a "moving" experience. So moving that my *profesora* asked if she could take it to share in the teacher's lounge. *"Si!"* I said. Yes, I was a stupid teenager.

Well, it was time for my payback. I was standing in Customs in Guatemala City, a day late, with only the clothes on my back, a handbook entitled *How to Learn Spanish in 30 Minutes a Day*, 5000 toothbrushes, and deflated balls! (Figuratively and literally!) Correction: 4850 toothbrushes. The guerilla soldiers inside the airport had helped themselves to their share.

Eventually, I was picked up by a missionary priest, who was my only point of contact in the country as I exited the airport into third-world urban chaos. It was my understanding that I would be helping young adults at a school in the city learn better English and assist with physical education.

After a short lunch, during which I chipped my tooth on a hamburger (burgers will never be the same), I discovered that plans had changed and I was needed at a new missionary outpost up in the mountains.

As our small, stick-shift pick-up truck ground its gears up the mountain road, I watched civilization fall away behind us. The sweltering, crowded, shop-lined streets, crammed with traffic and plumes of diesel fumes, became less congested and were replaced with lush, dark green foliage and cooler mountain air. My mind was overloaded with sights, sounds, and smells that were completely foreign to my being.

Urban smog was replaced with sporadic bonfire smells, mixed with a hint of burnt plastic, most likely from burning trash. Although we seemed to be in the middle of nowhere, with steep mountain slopes on either side of the gravel road, pedestrians lined the road, walking beside cars and trucks and motorcycles. I tried unsuccessfully to figure out where they were headed.

Colorfully painted "chicken buses," typical of Central America and so called because of their ability to carry large crates of market goods, searched for the next gears to chug to the higher elevations. Two such busses going opposite directions shared the narrow confines of the pedestrian-lined road without concern about the steep cliff falling away only inches from their tires.

After a seemingly endless ride along the mountainside, we turned off onto a worn side street that opened up into a village called Santo Tomás, Milpas Altas. The track was still congested with people, cars, trucks, and market goods. Everyone was intent on heading somewhere—and taking their own good time.

The cracked concrete street was lined with makeshift fences dividing various family plots of farmland. Having grown up in Wisconsin, with its vast agricultural acreage, I wondered how anyone could grow enough on these small parcels to survive or sustain a business. As we continued toward the center of town, one-story concrete shops and homes lined the roadway with only inches to spare.

Chickens darted to and fro beneath lines of laundry strung between the roofs. Scrawny street mutts nervously avoided people, while women were busy sweeping their stoops and throwing out buckets of water to keep the dust down.

The colonial influence was evident in the way that most all activity clustered around the central square, built of concrete and lined with scraggly bushes and ornamental trees. It seemed that concrete was something available in abundance in Guatemalan communities. Shops and homes were practically indistinguishable from one another, at least to my new-arrival eyes. Large steel doors, often large enough to drive through, marked some of the houses.

At one of the doors, I was literally dropped off, told, "Good luck, God bless, and call if you need anything." The cell phone had not yet been invented and there were no phone lines. I was told that the "*banditos*" (literally translated as "bandits") had stolen the copper wire in the phone lines to sell on the black market. I had never encountered a "bandit" before so not using the phone was just fine with me. Life had changed so much back home that there was nothing to want to call back to anyway.

The missionary church I was sent to had a Honduran priest who could speak (and cook) Italian, an interesting skill set in a Guatemalan village. He didn't know I was coming and he didn't have the Spanish version of "*How to Speak English in 30 Minutes a Day.*"

"*Padre,*" as I called him, was also the principal of the primary school where I was going to volunteer. Our first night was an international charades summit. It's amazing what you can communicate through body language and expressions.

Whether it's another language, a person with a disability, or even a child, practicing the art of communication without words is as humbling as it is empowering when the connection is made.

Because the house belonged to the attached church, it happened to be one of the larger abodes. It was a cold, concrete structure, but it was clean and I had my own room, which allowed me to talk to the walls when I needed to ask, "What the hell am I doing here?" that first night.

That question became even more apparent when Alberto, a teacher who was temporarily living there as well, showed me around my new home. It was a quick tour of the five-room house, which included the tiny kitchen and parlor. He enthusiastically showed me the indoor plumbing first, as if it were unexpected. I could only guess what his own home was like.

While I tried to comprehend why the toilet had no seat, he explained in lively Spanish the procedure of taking a shower. It would have made a great *Saturday Night Live* skit. I couldn't figure out if Alberto was trying to educate me on the art of taking a stand-up shower or if he was alluding to our having to conserve water by showering together. Luckily, I finally was able to understand, again through pantomime, that he was explaining about water pressure and that water was very scarce.

Before I could retire to my room to collapse after what had been a three-day journey, my priest-host had something else for me—clothes. My luggage had not gotten off the plane with me, so he generously loaned me some of his. He proudly offered a striped rugby shirt about three sizes too short and a pair of black polyester pants, also way too short for my six-foot-six tall frame, which I accepted gratefully. As I lay down on my too-short bed for the first time, I smiled to myself and thought how humbling this adventure was turning out to be already. I fell asleep before I could pull the threadbare covers over my exhausted body.

As daylight broke, I heard a pack of pigs walk past my bedroom, their squeals and hoof beats echoing off the cinderblock walls like I was in a subway. Then there was the ever-cocky rooster rattling my sleep. His cry would haunt me for months to come as a welcome to the cold mountain mornings.

Padre handed me a strong cup of coffee and a chunk of bread with mashed frijoles spread across it like peanut butter toast, and then beckoned me to follow him. As we entered the walled schoolyard next door, I saw a tiny Guatemalan boy in a school uniform jumping to ring the old school bell. As I looked around the meager, impoverished school grounds that butted up against the adjoining church's cemetery, I saw large, brown-eyed children's inquisitive looks follow me. Guatemalans are not exactly known for their height, and plump, little Guatemalan children are even more vertically challenged. There I was, standing six feet six inches tall with pale, white Irish skin. Let's just say, I stood out a bit.

I was led across the mud-packed playground with rain-filled potholes to one of four corrugated tin-roofed, cinderblock classrooms. Padre immediately greeted the children and began addressing the class with a version of Spanish seventeen times faster than my Spanish dictionary could keep up with. I guessed that he was talking about me, and unfortunately, I was right. When he was done, he handed me a marker for the only piece of technology the school had… a dry erase board. Then he said, "OK, teach!"

I still remember the awe in the eyes of the children crunched together in the one-light-bulb classroom, the appreciative eyes of Padre, and the curious eyes of the teacher whose curriculum I was about to disrupt for months to come. She had not planned for a non-Spanish-speaking, non-teacher to be thrown in front of her class.

The rest of the grade levels were clamoring to get a look at me through the crammed doorway and one dirty window. I was a deer in headlights. Time moved infinitesimally slowly, like the day my brother died.

"*What am I doing? I'm not a teacher. What did I get myself into? I don't even speak Spanish, for the love of God!*" Those were the thoughts that raced through my mind as my neck and face filled with the blood of embarrassment. I blinked, trying to make myself disappear. Years earlier, I had taught myself in a grade school magic act to escape from handcuffs in front of my class, but I never quite perfected the trick of making myself disappear.

For some reason, the defense mechanism that kicked in at that moment was laughter. The spirit of humor of how unreal this situation was ignited a wildfire in me. A new type of smile was born in me that day.

I gently said, "*Uno*," and used my body language and previous evening's charades to ask the children to repeat after me. They reciprocated, "*Uno*," with the same respectful, gentle voice. I then said, "One," to which they awkwardly responded "gwon." I then said, "*Dos*," with a little more confidence, to which they replied, "*Dos*," with similar confidence. I repeated the number in English, and they echoed my words. I then belted out, "*Tres*," which they followed with a louder, "*Tres*." I then overconfidently roared, "Three!" And that is when it happened. They roared back, "TREE!"

Could it be this easy? Could I be teaching and could they be learning?

That day, in a simple Guatemalan mountain village classroom, the teacher in me was born. The Guatemalan ancestors were the Maya. They had invented the calendar, but I had re-invented myself as a passionate educator.

I taught numbers, letters, colors, and simple phrases (all from my $4.95 *How to Speak Spanish in 30 Minutes a Day* handbook). When I wasn't teaching, I was taking the bus

My first classroom in Santo Tomás, Milpas Atlas, Guatemala

and walking around the market asking questions, making a fool out of myself, floundering through my Spanglish, an awkward blend of English and Spanish.

In the mornings, I taught kindergarten, which had my pace of simple language, minus the squeakiness of the children's voices. My plump little Guatemalan kindergarten students played a large role in being my saving grace. It was a trip back to the humble basics for me. The song and dance, tears and laughter, melted away my hardened exterior. This was the second time in only months that I welcomed the simple perspective of the world through a child's eyes.

Estuardo was the son of two of the most incredible human beings I have ever met. His parents were named Hugo and Lesbia. Looking back, Hugo and Lesbia were angels in couple form. They brought me into their family in an unconditional way that captured my heart.

Hugo filled my brother's shoes—he became the brother I had never had, for in fact, Joe had often been too busy or too cool to be a big brother. Hugo, on the other hand, loved learning all about me. He was a farmer, a husband, a father, a son, a volunteer teacher, a volunteer maintenance man around the school, and an active member of the church community.

My relationship with Hugo marked the beginning of my allowing others into my life to heal the wounds of lost love that were still festering. At every turn, Hugo greeted me with a huge smile and a helpful hand. He helped me with my Spanish, and I helped him with his English.

His wife and Estuardo's mother, Lesbia, was a beautiful Guatemalan woman with amazing patience and tenderness. Hugo and Lesbia's passion for life, their embrace of all who crossed their path, was the positive uplift I yearned for. I only hoped I could eventually match their pride for their children and love for one another.

Their son, Estuardo, was an extension of their joy. His huge brown eyes lit up the dark classroom with hope and wonder. Although all the children in the kindergarten immediately felt comfortable enough to climb all over me, Estuardo was proud that his parents were close friends of mine He was extra-patient with me as I learned new songs and struggled with my rudimentary Spanish.

I think it was Estuarado who first planted the seed in me that I might someday be a leader. His close relationship with me empowered him to become the three-and-a-half foot leader of the class. Sure, he had to compete with Gaby, another future leader. I watched with a grin on my face as Estuardo pulled up his slipping school uniform pants at the front of the class as if to say, "Get in line, everyone. I'm the teacher's right-hand man and it's coloring time!"

His tenderness and understanding were highlighted the day we read together. Sitting on my lap as I read a story about a turtle, he showed me that humility can be a good thing. The word "turtle" in Spanish is *tortuga*. When I read this word, the little boy looked up at me and gently grabbed my lips and said, "No, *Profe*" (short for professor) "*Tor – tuu – ga*" while he rolled the "r" with his tongue and moved my lips in hopes my tongue would mimic his. Learning to roll an "r" in the Spanish language took a bit of work. For *Taco* (me), it apparently also took fingers. My teacher that day was a four-year-old child.

The teach-the-teacher moments between child and grown man continued to evolve on a daily basis. The dose of humility and pure joy that entered my heart only fueled my desire to help the children even more. All of the education I had taken for granted for so many years started to spill out across the classrooms.

One evening, I discovered a drawer with simple pictures colored by the children. I wondered why they were in a drawer and not on the wall. I decided to let their efforts shine. When I posted the artwork, something magical happened. The kids arrived the next morning to cinderblock walls that were no longer barren. They were fascinated.

The kindergarteners took great pride in their creations. Each day, I put up their new drawings and began to watch an amazing transformation. The children began using more colors as their eyes widened with appreciation and pride. They started to color inside the lines with a deeper sense of care and concern. Their only limitations were the few colors the school could afford and the space on the walls.

To make room on the classroom walls for more artwork, I had the children write "*Te Amo*" ("I love you") on their creations and sent them home to their mothers. The following day, instead of the mothers dropping their children off at the outside school gate, they dropped them off at the classroom door. As they peered inside, a new look of interest filled their deep brown eyes. Their children's curiosity had spilled over onto the mothers. As I humbly looked through the eyes of a Guatemalan child onto what was once a blank canvas filled with possibility, I began to see how transformation could take place. One child at a time. One mother at a time. A mosaic of simple joy, born from a leap of faith and courageous humility.

My Guatemalan students in Santo Tomás,
Milpas Altas, Guatemala

CHICO'S STORY

In every school across the globe, there is one child who is strung just an octave above everyone else. Chico immediately intrigued me. He was one complex, little Guatemalan hombre. His passion for life, all things but learning, was evident in the way he wanted to be at the center of everything. If there was a ball game on the playground, he wanted to make the teams and score all the points. If there ever was an argument, he was front stage center, even if he had nothing to do with it, which was rare. He thrived on people's energy and was one of the most playful spirits I've ever encountered.

Chico was the type of person who is hard to stay mad at because he immediately wanted to win back any lost respect he may have caused. He would smile at you with a look of, "Come on, it's not that bad." Everything was water under the bridge with Chico. His work ethic around the school was that of the head maintenance man, but his attention to learning was not so industrious.

Chico never carried his *cuaderno* (notebook) home, and often was found in detention or some form of timeout. He very quickly was back to making pleasantries and amends with whatever teacher reprimanded him. He was a sort of watered-down version of Eddie Haskell from the old *Leave It To Beaver*, and lovable to me in a weird way.

I never met Chico's parents, nor rarely, if ever, did I see him eat—two strange observations. Lunch at the school for most kids was typically a chunk of bread with *frijoles—*

refried beans—spread on it like we use peanut butter. It was the more well-off, poor children (if that makes sense) who brought enough coins to school to purchase Orange Crush soda, dispensed in plastic sandwich bags and some Central American knockoff of Cheetos.

Chico played the role of Oliver Twist quite well. Beyond the playfulness, fierce competitive spirit, and innate leadership qualities, his dust-caked face revealed the years of struggle within him. Chico was my buddy. It wasn't too hard to gain his respect because I loved competitive sports as much as he did. The same elements in Chico that attracted him to competitive sports, equally repelled him from wanting, or allowing himself, to learn in the classroom.

One evening, I found myself humbled to the core. One of the teachers in the school ran a makeshift, four-stool bar out of the front of her house across the courtyard from the school. I had been invited over for an evening soda. A drunken man stumbled from the dark street outside past our open doorway. My host and her husband exchanged a pleasantry with him with a note of teasing. They knew him. Everyone in Santo Tomás knew each other.

Guatemalans are a hard-working, respectful, yet playful people. The drunk man stopped long enough to see inside and notice me. He came into the doorway, knocking his vodka bottle against the wall. It was his birthday. He slurred some initial words that I could not make out. I was a bit worried that I was attracting unwanted attention for my gracious hosts. Not everyone welcomes American *gringos* in Guatemala. The ongoing civil war had some deep roots with the politics of the United States. Trust in foreigners does not run deep.

A shot of vodka was poured for me although I was still confused. I quickly realized, as he started rambling on, that he was attempting to pay me a compliment. In broken Spanglish, he said, "My boy, Chico, is not an easy boy to raise. He dislikes going to school or doing any of his studies. But when "Teecher" (*referring to the word he heard from his son about me*) came, there was a change in his attitude toward school and learning. He wanted to go and do his studies. He now loves going to school. You see, I'm not a very good man, and not a very good father. I drive a bus when there is work, but I just want my son to have a life better than mine. Thank you, Teecher!" That was the best shot I've ever had.

The irony in my life, and in the pivotal life, is that although you may be the teacher, you are often taught by the least likely people. Chico and his father were two pivotal teachers who honored me with their hearts in such a way that I am humbled for life.

MOON RIVER

Speaking of humility, *The Pivotal Life* would not be any fun if there weren't some self-deprecating stories. Throughout my six months in Guatemala, my GI system was taken on a roller coaster ride. Some nights, I literally fell asleep on the toilet seat due to diarrhea. (Yes, I ended up buying a toilet seat for the house.) To this day, I don't know if what came out can even be called diarrhea. My intestines invented a new substance.

Digestive tract distress is a reality for foreigners who are not careful about what foods and drinks they consume. I was not able to be careful when everyone invited Padre and me to their homes for meals. He and I traveled extensively for house visits and dinners throughout his mountainous mission territory. Every place we went, we were offered food and "*No, gracias*" was not an option.

The only two "no thank you's" I ever pulled off in my time in Guatemala were my going-away party, when my students gave me animals as farewell gifts, and when a family tried to arrange a marriage with me and their daughter between the dinner's main course and dessert.

One of my most interesting meals was warmed, raw bacon between two pieces of bread. Maybe that explains how I lost twenty additional pounds from my already slender frame in a few weeks time. No matter what the cause, I found myself in a clinic getting an enema for a parasitic infection from two quite attractive Guatemalan nurses. None of us had woken up that morning thinking we would be in this reciprocal relationship. In fact, due to my clumsy Spanish and lack of Spanish medical lingo, I didn't even know they were performing an enema until the last moment. Maybe you could refer to that too as a "pivotal" moment.

I was so embarrassed that I actually reenacted the scene from the 1980s movie, *Fletch*, when Chevy Chase's character began singing *Moon River* abruptly, not knowing he would be receiving a prostate exam. Needless to say, the nurses and I all blushed.

This particular procedure, although I considered it more of a violation, required me to hold in the enema's medicated solution as "administered" until I arrived home, to give it time to work. I have never seen a priest laugh as much as Padre did during that ride home in his pick-up truck. The clinic was in Antigua, Guatemala, and the entire city is paved with colonial cobblestone streets strewn with potholes. I barely made it, but holy Moses, my humility blossomed in that clinic and bumpy streets that day.

It takes courage to laugh at yourself. Slimming down my ego while building up my character was just the right Central American diet for me at that point in life.

HUMILITY IN THE HUMIDITY

Although I'm convinced that humility is a key point on the compass of *The Pivotal Life*, it does not always come from heartfelt or embarrassing moments. Sometimes courageous humility comes from a space deep inside, only triggered in pivotal moments filled with sheer terror.

One such time I experienced terror, I had been invited to go on a weekend excursion with one of Padre's friends and his wife and teenage daughter from the city. We went to the tropical, black volcanic, sandy shores of the coast where many Guatemalans go for R&R.

In the evening, our driver, the teenage daughter, and I decided to leave the sleepy beachside cabanas. We walked to a nearby village in search of some entertainment. A cool beverage in the thick, sweaty, tropical air was entertainment enough. Many Guatemalan bars, if not all, outside of any metropolitan area, were makeshift counters that looked more like cheaply built, homemade, plywood workbenches.

I cracked open a Gallo beer and began quenching my thirst with its cool contents. A man took interest in me, as I stood out in the neighborhood, and struck up a conversation in English. We talked for some time until my Guatemalan friend was able to quietly tell me to disengage quickly. He said that the only people who spoke English in that community were cocaine dealers. Check, please!

The three of us started walking the half mile back into the dark streets that would eventually lead us to our beach cabanas. Note: Don't think beachside luxury; think wooden tents on an abandoned state beach campground with nothing around it. As we were walking, I had the "movie-like" feeling we weren't the only ones on the deserted, moonlit road. Oceanside communities such as the one we were on have few to no lights. Many homes have one or two light bulbs, if any. The road was more of a mud-packed path snaking through the jungle past tiny dark shacks of street-side homes. There had been enough moonlight to make everything have a grayish outline.

My gut feeling was confirmed when I saw a man between two shacks looking our way. Then another, and another, appeared. Before long, a number of these shady characters had converged behind us. We sped up our walk and so did they. Out of sheer anxiety, I picked up a baseball-sized rock as my only sense of protection. As an ex-college baseball pitcher, my throwing arm was my only strength and protection. My body's fight-or-flight mechanisms were competing in a tug-of-war. All I could think about at that moment was the same feeling of helplessness and despair I had felt when five men in a Denver alley jumped me one night in college. I had been pummeled, and I didn't want to feel that again.

I couldn't stop thinking about the safety of the teenage girl with us. It was then that I saw one of the most humbling objects I believe exists. I caught the glint off of a pistol in the hand of a very young boy right behind me, eight feet and closing. As if on autopilot, I placed my body between the teenage girl and the boy with the pistol. I whispered frantically to her to run and not look back. I must have spoken in English, but the tone in my voice translated perfectly well. In what kind of movie had I just found myself the brave, yet stupid, actor?

She took off and we sped up. At that point, we were almost to the small bridge that acted as the end of the village. The small mob escort service had apparently completed its mission. Their goal to intimidate us out of their territory was accomplished. Job well done! We had taken off running.

The following morning, I woke up practically on top of the four others I had traveled with. We had been sardined into the small cabana on the floor. My face, sweaty from the ridiculous humidity, was covered in ants and sand. What a way to end one of the most humbling experiences I have ever had—that is, until the following week.

PIONEERS OF TORTURE

It was a cool, damp morning, not unlike any other in Santo Tomás, when I woke up beneath a stitched, patched quilt, covered by a woven, Guatemalan-patterned blanket. My recent purchases were not thick enough to keep the incessant rooster's call to morning from reaching my ears like an annoying alarm clock set out of reach. I rolled out of the valley my heavy body had created in the 40-year-old mattress with what felt like knotted-up T-shirts. As I emerged from my cocoon of blankets, the cold, tiled floor of my Guatemalan mountain bedroom abruptly ended my warm dreams.

It was Day Two in my quest to retrieve boxes of supplies that had been sent a month earlier from friends back home in the States. Added to the long list of the things that don't happen as fast as I had grown accustomed to in the United States, was the tortoise pace of the Central American Postal Service. Days earlier, I had received word that a shipment consisting of a few boxes packed to the brim with arts and crafts supplies for my students was awaiting me in Guatemala City at the Customs Office.

The previous day, I had made the two-hour journey by truck down through the mountains to gather my packages. In the United States, a package, via the slow and cheap route, took only a week to be delivered, but then is dropped off at my doorstep. In Guatemala at that time, the packages took a month for delivery and required a two-hour drive, and what would be two days of standing in multiple lines, filling out forms, and obtaining countless stamps of approval from Customs. This lack of efficiency was the reality of a country still in the throes of a civil war.

After hours of waiting in lines for stamps of approval, and more ink than was contained in the markers in the packages, I had success. With accomplishment in my heart, I grew curious about the capital city that was the nerve center of the struggling country. There was a sign I had driven by four times over the past two days. It was a massive banner that hung on the wall of the city's military base. It read, *Pioneros de la Paz* (Pioneers of Peace). I had been told that behind the same wall upon which that banner hung proudly, a Catholic nun doing humanitarian work had been imprisoned and tortured with cigarette burns to her back.

Sometimes, I do not know what my fascination is with attempting to capture the human reality with my camera, but that day was one of them. I asked my driver if he could drive past the bannered wall slowly so that I could capture this symbol of corruption, abuse, and absolute farce, in my lens. He was terrified to do so, but out of respect and repeated requests, my wish was granted.

At worst, my camera would be confiscated and perhaps end up behind those walls. At best, I would have the banner documented in my journey to a land fraught with a past and present of human rights violations. Was it worth it? Hell, yes! If only for the tale to tell to build awareness with those who take for granted their liberties. It may only have been a photograph of a banner that appeared to promote a noble mission statement, but it will forever remind me of how propaganda fools the oppressed into a false sense of security. *Pioneers of Peace*—I think not—*Pioneers of Torture* would be a better fit.

THE SOLDIER

Shortly after my risky photographic adventure, my driver had an errand to run at a bank, so I walked around the capital city. Outside the police headquarters, which had once been a part of a beautiful cathedral, I noticed a small child, about two years old. He was physically distorted, clad only in an old diaper, sitting on the concrete sidewalk with a worn plastic dish placed between his nonfunctioning arms.

The plan for whatever desperate parent who placed him there was to collect a few centavos (pennies) from sympathetic passersby. There were literally hundreds of people practically stepping over the child, hardly noticing his place on the earth. I don't know what was worse—that no one noticed him, or that someone, some *thing*, had placed him there on the side of the street to collect money. I stopped and stared. For the life of me, I could not see anyone in the vicinity who could be remotely responsible for this child. I wasn't horrified, but rather, astonished. I couldn't take my eyes off the boy.

I witnessed poverty and injustice every day in a land torn by civil war, much of which has seared itself into my soul, but that was unimaginable. In the States, I live in a world where I attend fundraising dinners of elite philanthropists and compassionate citizens who give their time and wealth to the marginalized. However, their generosity is usually to an organization rather than given directly to an individual. Outside of possibly volunteering at a soup kitchen, in the U.S., most philanthropic efforts do not engage with actual forgotten and abandoned persons on the streets of a Third World country. The dichotomy between these two methods had me reflecting for years on how disconnected—though nevertheless still important—a charitable donation might be. There is no right or wrong, but the perspective that can be gained from interacting face to face with the less fortunate, rather than simply through a fundraising effort, is what was most eye-opening for me.

Before I could process the human drama I was experiencing firsthand, I noticed one character hovering high above the child. It was a soldier. He was armed with an old machine gun and a stoic stare similar to one of the Buckingham Palace guards. This soldier almost looked as if he were protecting the child I had mentally adopted. I questioned whether his military power represented what was wrong with Guatemala. Was he the symbol of the past 30-plus years of human rights violations? Or was he something more, a man with his own child, practically forced to wear the uniform of power and oppression, showing his true humanity, watching out for this child who could not care for himself?

The image of the soldier and child could have been on the cover of *Time Life* magazine; it spoke to the volumes of injustices of millions, and highlighted the 150,000 people who "disappeared" throughout the civil war in Guatemala due to genocide.

Over the years, that Guatemalan soldier, has become closely related to another historic soldier who has captivated my mind—the Roman soldier at the foot of the cross of Jesus in biblical Scripture. I have always wondered about that Roman soldier and what went through his mind to make his tremendous transformation. The Roman authorities must have used their strongest, most trained soldiers, to guard the activities of the crucifixion that day, in fear of protests and mobs. The soldier in the account would have been as mentally tough and dedicated as was his brute nature.

In the historical account of the Bible, after Jesus was crucified and turned his life over to death, a Roman soldier knelt before the cross and said, "Surely this was the Son of God." The Guatemalan soldier, approximately two millennia later, representing another dictatorship, seemed to be standing before the helpless Guatemalan child. I asked myself, "Was this Guatemalan soldier just moments away from the same transformation that had taken place with his Roman counterpart? Would he too have a change of heart? Would his perspective change? And maybe it already had. *Who am I to judge?* My mind continued to wonder.

I had grown up hearing biblical stories, but this "pivotal" moment made it all so real. Was I meant to witness that scene, to be an observer of an injustice that caused a softening of the heart, or simply to learn from it? Was this moment meant to be a spiritual awakening to what I was called to be—a protector or message-bearer of the abandoned, forgotten, and marginalized? Maybe this pivotal moment was simply the universe's smelling salts to wake me up to the world surrounding me. Was the experience a beckoning to look at what was beneath me (the oppressed who get walked over) and toward the powers-that-be, above me (the authority, those who have the power to protect or destroy)?

Pivotal moments have the power to move us in directions that are at first unimaginable, yet the characters and experiences are images and realities all around us. We don't need a camera to capture them, nor an explanation or understanding, only an openness to stop and let them touch our heart. Once this happens, something much bigger than you or me takes over and motivates us to move forward with an even keener awareness. This newfound sensitivity will guide us on our own unique paths.

Blessed are they who see beautiful things in humble places
where other people see nothing.
—Camille Pissaro

I do not believe that an injustice should dictate that we act in one certain way out of some guilt and obligation. If we are all indeed "snowflakes," according to my mother, not one like the other, then we each have some unique gift to add to the world. Maybe one person will change the child's diaper, one will place money into his plastic dish, one will become an ethical soldier standing guard, another an advocate for the poor, or another, an advocate for the disabled.

That day, for me, it was none of those. I think back to that boy often and wish I had done more. The experience has seeped into my soul over the years, and perhaps made me more perceptive of the images and people I walk past every day of my life. To live *The Pivotal Life* is to see with an open mind and an open heart, to be humbled by the human drama, and to learn from it.

An old woman scavenging for something to sell in Central America's largest landfill in Guatemala City

Whether confronting the helplessness of someone dying in my arms or the humility encountered almost daily in a foreign land such as Guatemala, I was learning invaluable lessons. *The Pivotal Life* is not a life filled with certainty and confidence. It is a life of smallness and little control out in the open water. The waves will take you where the waves will take you. Humility becomes your lifesaver. It allows you to rise above your pride.

The key to *The Pivotal Life* is to allow yourself to experience new things. Your humble approach to your new surroundings announces to others that you do not have all the answers, but rather, that you seek to understand more, to reach further. This takes courage.

Humility is the strength that is often underestimated in our success-driven culture. I think the poet Tennyson had it right when he said that humility is, "… the highest virtue, the mother of them all."

REFLECTION QUESTIONS

- What is one humbling experience you have had?
- What did you learn from it?
- Are you able to find humor in humbling moments?
- Think of a time you impacted a child's life.
- Name a moment when an unexpected person impacted your life.

NOTES

WISDOM

Welcomed to Oz with open arms

THE GREAT OZ WITHIN

Knowing yourself is the beginning of all wisdom.
—Aristotle

After six months in Guatemala gaining perspective on my humble place in the world, I traveled to the other side of the planet to continue my journey. Guatemala had only scratched the surface. I wanted to experience more of what this swirling mass of life had to offer. I knew education was key, so I found a way to accomplish both—continue college and become a student of life. I used some money from my brother's college fund to attend a study-abroad program in Australia, a.k.a. "Oz." After the semester ended, I backpacked through the Australian Outback. Hundreds of miles from the nearest civilization, I found myself in a pivotal moment, discovering that wisdom can arise in uncommon ways.

During my time exploring the natural wonders of Oz, I joined up with a guided expedition in Kakadu National Park. Over seven thousand square miles of raw nature in all its glory. My group included four Europeans and an Aussie guide named Deeno. By dawn of the second day, I knew we had an unconventional (somewhat crazy) guide. One of his many eccentric ways was that he refused to don any footwear in what is some of the harshest environment in the Australian outback. Deeno's interpretation of the national park's rules seemed to suit Deeno more than common sense or safety.

The first night, after setting up camp, Deeno sent me to collect a bucket of fresh water for cooking from the nearby river. He told me to wade out into the middle of the moonlit river, where the water was supposedly cleaner.

After stepping out of my hiking boots and peeling off my socks, I carefully walked into the silent, black water with a bucket in hand. When I reached knee-deep water, I leaned over to allow fresh water to flow into the bucket.

Although the cool evening river water felt refreshing on my legs and feet, dusty and sweaty from the day's safari, I felt a presence in the water that began to make me suspect that I wasn't the only one there. Recall the Guatemalan ocean-side village story? It was an innate sense that pushed me back to shore, the now-heavy bucket splashing in rhythm with my feet sloshing through the water. As in any Hollywood drama, it appeared that it was just my mind playing tricks on me—or so I thought.

In the morning, when I returned to the shore to wash up, I saw an old sign posted about 20 feet from where I had been wading in the river the night before. It announced, "NO SWIMMING—CROCS." Crocodiles are some of the largest and most ferocious man-eaters that slither the planet, and they are abundant in the Australian wild. At that moment, I felt one part powerless and one part grateful that I had not been a meal the night before.

Later that day, we went upriver to take a boat to watch the same crocs the sign had warned about. The locals call them "jumpers" because of how they launch their 14-foot bodies out of the water to feed. We tied dead chickens to the ends of long poles to view how the crocs could jump from a swimming position. I appreciated their awesome power and agility more than ever, knowing that I had foolishly and naively shared that same feeding ground the previous evening.

WISDOM FROM ABROAD

The same trusted guide who had sent me into the dangerous river the night before, had the group scale the brittle wall of a steep, narrow gorge. The climb was hand over foot, which I accomplished by watching the bare, dusty feet of our fearless leader ahead of me. Deeno's expedition was growing more hardcore by the second.

At the top of our five-story perch, Deeno shoved his backpack into my arms. Just as quickly, he launched his scrawny, tanned body off the cliff to plummet into the cold waters below. This was not the ordinary cliff jump I was familiar with from my Canadian Boundary Waters trips as a teen. Here, any daring cliff-jumper would have to hurl himself far enough out to clear the rock ledge three stories below, but not so far as to slam into the sheer rock wall on the opposite side of the gorge. Either scenario—coming up too short or propelling oneself too far, would have a net result of something awful, if not devastating.

At that moment, though, I didn't care about any of those trivial facts. All I could think about was how cool Deeno's jump had been, and how mine *would* be. I wanted to follow suit more than life itself. It would be a coming of age moment, like getting a tattoo, that would mark me for life. It would be bravery, beauty, and sheer testosterone in one single leap.

My fellow travelers from the European Union had also been awed by Deeno's leap of insanity, but not enough to prevent them from chanting "JUMP, JUMP, DO IT!" in my ear as they realized I was making my ready. The Greek Sirens lured me to the edge in fascination. Everything in my being wanted to jump, even though my legs were quivering like the first time I had spoken in front of a large audience as a child. Even though my gut was saying "NO!" my adrenaline-filled mind was saying, "HELL, YES!"

For some unknown reason, on a steep Australian cliff in the middle of nowhere, on the other side of the world, I heard a distant voice from my past. It was my father's voice saying, "Jeff, what do you have to prove?" A man with whom I had rarely seen eye to eye while growing up saved my life that day.

I did not jump. Sometimes wisdom blossoms at just the right moment.

It is a wise father who knows his own child.
—William Shakespeare

Now, as a parent myself, I have a far greater appreciation for the things that I try to instill in my children, even if they do not seem to hear what I say. Whether you are currently a parent, or hope someday to become one, when you love someone, you plant seeds of wisdom, no matter the rocky terrain. You can only hope those seeds take root, grow, and blossom at just the right time.

The Pivotal Life is one that is supported by the wisdom of our mentors and those who care for us. Although the journey is often taken alone, we have free access to sage advice that can be a beacon calling out to us to live well.

Whenever life presents us with challenging moments, there is an inner voice nurtured by parents, teachers, coaches, or mentors we can tap into for strength, endurance, and discernment. Often we avoid these voices out of stubborn independence or simple ignorance. Our inner wisdom calls out to connect with other sage advice when we don't know what direction to pivot. Those who want to live *The Pivotal Life* must welcome the lifesaver aid to be best prepared for everything presented to us by life itself.

REFLECTION QUESTIONS

- Name some wise people in your life whom you have turned to.

- How often do you search for sage advice during life's pivotal decisions?

- What can we do to develop relationships with wise people so that they are there when we need them?

NOTES

BELIEF

An Attitude Adjustment

Be faithful in small things
because it is in them that your strength lies.
—Mother Teresa

Jennifer and I were blessed with the pregnancy of our second child in 2006. There are not many things as joyful as the anticipation of a new child whom you have created. The immediate sensation of fatherly pride overwhelmed me. I had been ecstatic about my first child, but "Round Two" was an opportunity to grow my legacy. I was pumped!

Jennifer was on a work trip to Chicago eleven weeks into the pregnancy when she felt cramping and fell over onto the hotel's bathroom floor, bleeding severely. That was far too sensitive an experience to detail, yet the terror it must have caused her is something a father can never quite appreciate. She was rushed to the hospital, where she awaited news that she might have miscarried.

We knew that there were some, not uncommon, concerns with our little peanut staying attached to Mom's uterus. But reality approached as she was wheeled into the ER.

Through all the pain and blood, there a tiny heartbeat. Our peanut had hung on. His adventure was only beginning. Over the coming months, each and every ultrasound showed a worsening situation. The subchorionic hematoma (which was like a blood bubble between the baby and mother) continued to grow larger and larger.

We were sent to a prenatal specialist who confirmed the grim news. The perinatologist matter-of-factly told us to expect a second trimester "event." "Event," was defined as a miscarriage or a pre-mature birth with the high probability of birth defects. The specialist told us, "It will not be a 'tax payer'." After all, a taxpayer must work, and if you are not alive, or are mentally challenged, you often do not pay taxes. That day, we changed the baby's name from "It" to "Jonah."

Jennifer was placed on strict bed rest four and a half months away from the due date. Hang in there, Jonah! Hang in there, Mom! Jennifer was a marathon runner. Her sitting in bed for so long, only to move to a couch, must win some kind of award for character and patience. Although pregnancy has its high and low points, I have to admit, that in my eyes, his mother's inner strength was a high point. She handled the bed rest with elegance and grace.

One day, during her bed rest, I was making a call on a doctor for my job. At that time, I was a pharmaceutical representative selling medications. The doctor greeted me in the hallway between patients to sign for medicine samples. The majority of the doctor's patients lived below the poverty line and free medicine samples were vital to their health and wellness.

The doctor pleasantly asked how I was doing. I replied, "Not bad considering my new job, a one-year-old child at home, and a wife on bed rest." He was intrigued and asked for more details. When I told him about the pregnancy and prognosis, he nonchalantly told me, "Cut your losses, Jeff. It will surely slow you and your wife down."

Have you ever had an out-of-body experience, followed by a sense of being the proverbial deer in the headlights of a Mack truck going 70 mph? That was me.

The doctor continued advising me as to how a baby with special needs would hamper Jennifer and me from doing all the things we may want to accomplish in life. He even shared that he had a disabled brother whom his family took to famous religious sites to pray for a miracle, to no avail.

As he was talking, his next patient came down the narrow hallway. It was a young Latina mother pushing her disabled child in a stroller. The child was severely disabled, both cognitively and physically, as evidenced by the child's drooling and significantly spastic movements. The doctor pointed toward the child and said, "Here is an example now." I couldn't believe what I was witnessing. I respect life, but I also have been raised, and trained through my work, to respect a learned doctor's opinion. I walked out of his office in a daze.

That night, I couldn't tell Jennifer what had happened, and I surely couldn't sleep, so I started to do something I hadn't done in years … I put pen to paper. By early morning, I came to a conclusion.

I felt compelled to communicate a father's perspective, something I don't think is shared enough. Mothers seem to be so much better at expressing their thoughts and feelings, but this was one of those pivotal moments in life when I found myself struggling and wanting to share with others which path I felt compelled to journey down. Then I emailed my story to a couple of local newspapers before Jennifer even awoke.

I wrote, "Life shouldn't be predetermined by my needs to have an 'easy' life.... I am not sure what is in store for Jonah and us these next weeks, but to think of anything less than allowing God's plan to unfold in this beautiful, yet challenging, moment of creation, would be unconscionable. If Jonah crawls back into God's hands from his mother's womb, or if he crawls prematurely and awkwardly into our human arms, I will know that life was given a chance to exist, unhindered by any act of self-centeredness. This doctor, this shortsighted man, missed the miracle he sought for his own brother. If I could only get up every day and dress my struggling child like the dedicated and loving Latina mother, I would be a participant in one of the greatest miracles of all... LIFE."

As the weeks progressed, we X'd off the days on the calendar, hoping to get to the stage of development where Jonah could survive on his own if his mother went into pre-term labor. It was an emotional tug of war between hoping for the baby and distancing ourselves from him, knowing we most likely would lose him. I felt like it was a slow-motion miscarriage. We put off decorating his nursery.

When Jonah made it past 24 weeks, I headed for the toy store. His mother had decided on a safari theme for his room, so I went all out. I went up and down the aisles with huge stuffed animals to decorate the best safari-themed nursery I could dream up. I must have looked silly carrying a five-foot giraffe with other large, furry jungle creatures under my arms and wrapped around my neck. I was a proud papa!

Jonah not only went the distance of a full pregnancy, he went an extra two days! Born on January 30, weighing 8 pounds, 13 ounces, measuring 21 inches long, Jonah and Mom were in perfect health.

> *The truth is that our finest moments are most likely to occur when we are feeling deeply uncomfortable, unhappy, or unfulfilled. For it is only in such moments, propelled by our discomfort, that we are likely to step out of our ruts and start searching for different ways or truer answers.*
> —M. Scott Peck

With each hug I give Jonah as I cherish his life, I think he grows stronger and taller. Ironically enough, he is anything but delayed or physically challenged. He is heads and shoulders taller than kids his age. He plays baseball competitively against older kids. His strength is a testament to my

Jonah, my little superman

faith and dedication to our Creator's plan. Jonah's life proves that the doctor, who advised us to abort his life for the sake of our convenience, was wrong. I can never put myself in someone else's shoes, but I think that patience and belief guided me to the right choice.

Belief is not hope, rather, it is a deep conviction fueled by possibility. My belief in Jonah opened the door to many more possibilities in life that seem to be out of my control.

Whenever Jonah makes me a cup of coffee in the morning, or reminds me during a crazy, busy day that we forgot to pray before bed or a meal, I am humbled beyond measure as to how little we actually "control" in this life.

When you truly believe in someone, something, or yourself, you are rooted in such commitment that the risk of pain grows exponentially. For every success story like Jonah's birth, there are ten, twenty, or a thousand more that have more challenging, if not unfortunate, outcomes. Belief is knowing that things may not turn out how we might like them to, but pushing forward anyway.

Think of things you believe in and then take a moment to reflect on what if they took a turn for the worse. If you believed you did everything possible to prepare for a presentation and that it would be a success, and it turned out to be a flop, you would be crushed. If you believed you loved someone and that person disappeared, you would be left paralyzed. Belief is pushing forward even in the light of risk.

* * * * *

People are often unreasonable,
irrational, and self-centered.
Forgive them anyway.

If you are kind,
people may accuse you of selfish, ulterior motives.
Be kind anyway.

If you are successful,
you will win some unfaithful friends
and some genuine enemies.
Succeed anyway.

If you are honest and sincere,
people may deceive you.
Be honest and sincere anyway.

What you spend years creating,
others could destroy overnight.
Create anyway.

If you find serenity and happiness,
some may be jealous.
Be happy anyway.

The good you do today,
will often be forgotten.
Do good anyway.
Give the best you have,
and it will never be enough.
Give your best anyway.

You see, in the final analysis,
it is between you and God.
It was never between you and them anyway.

—Attributed to Mother Teresa
* * * * *

onah has continued to teach me about belief. It was a summer day after I had returned from leading a service trip overseas through my servant leadership program, Pivotal Directions.

One day, I was watching Jonah battle waves in a massive tidal wave pool called Poseidon in the Wisconsin Dells. I couldn't believe that Jonah's strong, seven-year-old body had once hung in limbo, before he had even taken his first breath. One torrid swell after another he faced head on with fierce excitement, being hurled through the gigantic waves in a mass of adult swimmers.

By late afternoon, my kids and I had traded the commercialized amusement water park for a more rustic, traditional, camping experience, just on the outskirts of the Dells. Jonah and his siblings ran for the lakefront water play area. I took a seat on a bench on shore in the last of the afternoon warm, golden sunshine. It was a simple paradise with an eighty-foot floating, rubber playground anchored in the shallows of the roped-off lake. From my bench, I could see only the dark outlines of children jumping from one rubberized raft section to the other in the bright sun dancing off the water. Screams of joy echoed around the lake and the neighboring marina.

Even with sunglasses, I couldn't make out which silhouettes were my kids. I would check in from time to time, calling out if everything was OK. I could see my daughter, Cecilia, and son, Bailey, but Jonah was missing in the sun-filled splashes around the metropolis of the water playground. I yelled out, asking where their brother was.

They didn't know. My first thought was that he was hiding from them or had found something more interesting than a constant chase of a little brother.

I yelled again, this time elevating my voice just a bit telling them to find him. No luck. I yelled louder, "Jonah?" Still no response. I yelled even louder, as my concern heightened. When Jonah did not appear, I began wading into the water, more frustrated than worried. A mother joined me, sloshing through the water at my side, also in her clothes. Maybe there was something in my voice that evoked her innate mother's fear.

As we grew closer and the silhouettes turned into people, Jonah was not one of them. I started shouting for everyone to help find my son. When that did not seem to help, I began pushing the moveable floating rafts as far as their anchors permitted. My shouts turned into demands for everyone to clear out of the water.

I crashed around the back of the floating playground, yelling Jonah's name even louder. My voice bounced off the water and disappeared into the nearby waterfront, wooded campsites. It was a hollow echo, as there were no more splashing children, only stunned onlookers from shore curious as to what was going on.

Still nothing. My screams picked up in fervor and seemed to have come from deeper inside. The water was only four feet deep, not high enough to cover Jonah's head.

"Call 911!" I heard someone yell in the distance. Or was it my own frantic voice?

"No, this cannot be happening!" I said under my breath. My relaxing vacation had done a 180-degree turn to become terror. My heart was sinking by the second. So much time had passed.

I desperately turned my search underwater. I started diving down into the murky water, using my long arms as my sight to find his body. When the air in my lungs was exhausted, I would come up gasping. As soon as I sucked in another breath, I would scream again with all a father's might, "JONAAAAAAH!" My voice bellowed in a way that silenced the marina, the shore, the campsites, and even the wildlife. Everything slowed down and became silent.

"This cannot be happening!" I cried inside. Back underwater, I roamed around, praying that I would find his body in time to administer CPR. I started hating myself for being a terrible father. I was a single father, recently divorced, and just trying to spend some quality time to show my kids how much I loved them. I had failed.

Back underwater, my mind fought, "No, he's gone. It's my fault." I still prayed for him to somehow be alive.

"I must BELIEVE," I battled back in my head. I had prayed for him to survive before he had even taken his first breath during that complicated pregnancy, and I prayed again that he could take one more breath. "Please, God! Please!" I said gasping for air.

From behind my gasping and moaning of gut-wrenching sounds, as shock was knocking on my door, I heard somebody yelling to me. From shore, I heard a voice yelling to me. Something, "… him."

Then, when it was repeated, I heard the word, "… found …"

I finally deciphered the words: "We found him!"

At that moment, I wasn't happy or relieved. I was dazed and confused. I wouldn't snap out of my nightmare until some visual confirmed the words I was hearing. I kept hearing myself repeat the words, "What? Where?"

"He's in the outhouse," someone said.

"Huh?" I replied.

"He's pooping!" my daughter laughed matter-of-factly.

"No way!" was my response.

Dripping wet, I ran up the campground road and met my stunned son. My look brought him to the border of tears and fright. The poor kid. He just had to go to the bathroom. I couldn't shake my fear, but I hugged him anyway with all my strength.

My belief in Jonah had been tested twice in drastic fashion in seven years. I hope I go the rest of my life not feeling that level of despair for any of my loved ones. However, despair needs belief. Belief is the requisite for climbing out of despair and staying out of its clutches.

In both pivotal moments I had with Jonah, my belief was strengthened and led me to a better appreciation of *The Pivotal Life*. It is a life worth risking lost love to climb to the higher branches that bear better fruit.

Today, Jonah is content and happy with jump shots, touchdowns, and home runs. *The Pivotal Life* is believing the impossible is possible.

REFLECTION QUESTIONS

- How do you define *belief* in your life?
- What guides you to press forward?
- Where do you turn, or who do you turn to, when the seas of life grow rough?

NOTES

HONOR

WEATHERED SKIN

Who sows virtue reaps honor.
—Leonardo da Vinci

"Mr. Thomas, would you like a shave and cut this morning?" I asked.

"Ya, Mon!" rang back at me in a Jamaican spirited tone expected of someone years younger.

His face lit up as he pulled his long hand across his unshaven cheek. He could have been a rich man on Wall Street in that moment, getting his face shaved, hair cut, and shoes polished, while reading how well his stocks were doing. It didn't matter that he was one of a hundred abandoned residents in Mother Teresa's Home for the Dying on a forgotten street in the Caribbean city of Kingston, Jamaica. Today, he would feel important.

In 1950, Mother Teresa founded a religious order of nuns to care for the poorest of the poor, those forgotten and abandoned on the streets of Calcutta, India. The nuns of the Missionaries of Charity care for lepers, orphans, and the dying. Their mission has spread across the globe. I first encountered these compassionate, committed hearts at their Home for the Dying in Kingston while leading a group of undergraduate students as part of my work with Boston College.

The home was a two-story concrete fortress of love. Although everything about the building was basic, down to the folding chairs and card tables, the nuns, in their spotless, white habits and serene faces, filled the cold concrete environment with care and compassion. The volunteer group I was leading was there as an extension of the dedicated hands of the founder, Mother Teresa. Our goal was to attempt to offer the same dignity to those at the end of their lives.

Moments earlier, I had timidly approached the aged, skinny man sitting in the sunlight against a pale blue, concrete wall in the courtyard. There was less of a dying look on his face than some strange smirk that he knew something I did not. It was "serenity," I think I noticed.

It wasn't until I had already committed in my mind to engaging him with the proposition of a shave that I noticed his blindness from severe cataracts. I could have pivoted to the left and approached a less disabled individual, one who could see and with all his limbs, but I honored my commitment.

But what was vision? I would soon find out.

A pleasant nun who worked at the home for the abandoned and dying had given me the names of a few of the men sitting quietly, almost motionless, in the sunlight against the concrete walls of the courtyard. My gut had taken me to the blind Mr. Thomas and I would stay with him. There was loyalty in my heart to go where my initial intuition took me.

When the aged residents were not in the meal hall or in bed, they were placed in the courtyard for a bit of fresh air and sunshine. This allowed their caretakers to clean the inside facilities, change linens, and tidy up the meal hall. By the time everything was washed to spotless condition, it would again be time to move the men back inside for the next meal. It was a constant cycle of cleaning.

I guessed there were two reasons for all the cleaning. The first was for sanitation reasons. There seemed to be no foul smell or flies in the otherwise decaying world. The second reason, which lent itself to the first, was for sake of dignity. The guiding philosophy of the Missionaries of Charity is to provide every human dignity, even if abandoned on death's doorstep. Until you have experienced the dignity with which those special angels cloaked in nuns' habits care for others, you haven't witnessed unconditional love.

Most of the residents at this location had been abandoned in some manner. Some were left to die on the streets, some in hospitals, and some simply could not be cared for any longer by their families due to extreme poverty and lack of resources. All they had left in the world was a group of tireless, faithful nuns as caretakers, inspired by Mother Teresa's tremendous love. The nuns tend to the weathered souls with love, bathe them with love, clothe them with love, pray with them in love, and shelter them with love.

There are few places on earth that exemplify the vast canyon of humility between giving and receiving as in that home for the dying. The nuns give with tremendous, unconditional love to the forgotten and abandoned, and the residents accept the care with an equal amount of humility, being utterly dependent on their caregivers.

As I prepared to shave Mr. Thomas, I realized I was out of my league. I was the polar opposite of Mr. Thomas. I was 25 with firm skin and soft, short stubble that was quite easy to shave. Mr. Thomas's beard was as stiff as wire bristles and embedded in the cracks of his leathery, weathered skin. It felt more like a first attempt at surgery than a quick, refreshing shave. I was relieved he could not see me as I investigated his face, trying to determine where best to begin and at what angle.

I had brought with me rubber medical gloves to stay clean out of fear that someone might have a disease. I pulled them off as soon as I put them on, feeling that they were an obstacle in reaching my goal—providing dignity. I wanted to treat Mr. Thomas with the same dignity that the nuns offered him on a daily basis. I was connecting with another human being, who just happened to have been forgotten by the world. Surely, I could safely shave his beard without the need of some medical gloves. I knew I would not want someone to touch me with rubber gloves.

What at first was my timid scratching away a few whiskers at a time, turned into less of a shave and more of an intimate experience. I had never been this close to another man's face, especially a stranger's. As a child, when my father went a day without shaving, which was rare because of his executive position, he would give me whisker kisses by rubbing his cheek against mine. I would watch him shave from afar in the bathroom mirror and imitate his facial movements that changed with each stroke of the razor. I would make an "O" with my mouth while stretching my neck into the air, as he did, followed by a pat of my cheeks, marking completion.

That day, I found myself on the small island of Jamaica, in the sprawling city of Kingston, holding a dying man's face, giving him a fresh look, one that he would never see, but one he could feel with his wizened and gnarly fingers. His ability to accept my compassion for him is something hard to put into words. In fact, we hardly spoke during our time together. Sometimes there is no need for words.

What should have taken several minutes became a half hour of navigating his wrinkled skin. All I had in hand was a cheap, overused disposable razor that seemed as ancient as its customers. Like everything else in this care facility, items were used to their full capacity. The razor had been dulled by countless uses. With a cloth dipped in a shallow plastic dish of cool water, I gently wiped away the foamy shaving cream, now embedded with bristly whiskers. It felt like I had completed a surgical procedure when we were done.

The fresh shave had uncovered his weathered skin. It was as if a thick fog had rolled away from a virgin ocean coastline. His life story had been exposed. The years of struggle could be seen like the circles depicting the life cycle of a cut tree trunk. However, I was the one with a new look, a new outlook. I wanted to learn more about living from this dying man.

To receive more, I must give more, I thought. I felt that I had now earned the privilege of offering Mr. Thomas a massage. He accepted.

First, I applied lotion to his one remaining hand—the other had been amputated years before. The smooth lotion quickly disappeared into the dry, rough, cracked skin, like water into an arid riverbed. I wondered what trials and tribulations his strong hand must have encountered throughout his long life.

Again, I thought of my own father, and the grandfather I had never met. My father has soft hands, not from an easy life, but rather, from one that worked tirelessly in the business world with paper and pen.

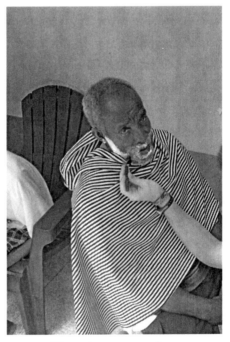

Honoring one another

I sat with a similar admiration of Mr. Thomas. It reminded me of my childhood hours doing my homework in my father's office, admiring him.

For the first time in my life, I found myself in a position to physically provide relief for an elder's hard work. Each time I rubbed lotion into Mr. Thomas' cracked hand, it was a sign of gratitude and respect. I was expressing my gratitude for being welcomed into his personal space. It was gratitude for the life he had lived. I have used the cliché before that "life is a journey, not a destination." I was living it. Instead of a handshake or high five for making it so far in his journey to the end of life, I was grateful for becoming part of that journey. It was also gratitude for his humility; he had become a pivotal character in the story of my life.

After the cracked skin of his hand had darkened as it absorbed the welcome lotion, I felt I had earned the right to go further and perhaps relieve more of his pain. I did not ask for permission at the time. I simply began to gently rub lotion into his bony arms, which had lost the strength of life. He sighed as I carefully pressed my fingers into muscles he hadn't felt in a long time. His muscles had atrophied, but his spirit was growing.

As I moved to his remaining limbs, I felt as if I were offering my strength to his. When I came to his single foot, I had truly entered a realm of humility unparalleled to any I had ever felt. The shave had been an intimate experience, but massaging his foot was an expression of pure humility. It was a process that needed to go in that order for me, from intimacy to humility, and back again to an even deeper sense of intimacy.

My sense of obligation to help the poor had long since evaporated, as had the lotion into his dried pores. My feeling of respect and desire to understand more pushed me past his long, overgrown, yellowed toenails and leathery, sandpaper foot. I was no longer timid in my approach. My spirit was eager to relieve the harshness upon which his foot had journeyed.

By the time the massage ended, we both had softened our exteriors together. We had allowed each other to give and receive one another while a new perspective was born. I believe my ability to honor Mr. Thomas as a valuable human being created just enough space that two strangers could come together and help and learn from one another. It in turn, would help me grow a step closer to offering myself to others. Who was the one in need that day?

"I was blind, but now I see."

A blind man gave me sight.

REFLECTION QUESTIONS

- Has your caring for another person caused you to look at your life differently?

- What prevents you from stepping outside of your comfort zone?

- Where could you find a Mr. Thomas in your life?

NOTES

REFLECTION

SILENCE SPEAKS LOUDLY

The unexamined life is not worth living.
—Socrates

D ays before my graduation from Marquette University in Milwaukee, Wisconsin, I dropped in on a dear Jesuit friend of mine, Frank. I was freaking out! I would be giving the baccalaureate speech at graduation in front of thousands of my classmates and their families, reflecting on what the years at Marquette had given us, and how it had prepared us for the world. I was meant to send my class forth into the world to seize the day. Trouble was, I had no clue what I was to do with my own life.

My friend simply told me in his own unique way to chill and when the graduation was over, to consider going to the New Camaldoli Hermitage on the mountainous cliffs of Big Sur, California, to retreat in contemplative silence with the monks. *What?! Me?!*

I'm the kind of person who needs to talk to process life and all its decisions. Why would someone who knew my personality so well tell me to do the opposite and shut up? I went back to my apartment and stared from my bed at the ceiling for hours asking myself this silly question. Why was it so alluring?

ook seventeen years for me to take Frank up on his recommendation. Time is an interesting thing, isn't it? I had come to the understanding that my life was pulled in many directions. I had been so hyper-focused on career, relationships, my children, and my outside interests that I had lost my true focus. Sure, all these things were important, but as the late, great, Green Bay Packer football coaching legend, Vince Lombardi, once said about priorities: "God, family, and the Green Bay Packers, in that order."

I had lost focus on my core, who I was. I had my priorities out of order.

On my trips, I tell my students that you cannot be a good leader of others until you lead yourself. How can I be whole to others, a man of service, unless I am whole and true to myself? Life is all about balance. I had heard this dozens of times. Our cars need tune-ups, runners need rest, and houses need spring cleaning, but we fragile human beings, built of a complex mix of emotional, spiritual, physical, cognitive, and relational moving parts, often ignore the need for a break.

Just as Lombardi realized, half-times and off seasons are not only for rest, but to reflect on the past in order to be more efficient in the future. Frank, who had become like a coach to me, as well as a friend, confidante, and mentor, saw that I was going a million miles an hour, albeit successfully, but that for me to find my center, my purpose, and perspective, I needed to retreat to a place where the Spirit could speak to me. Not only would it be important to locate a venue and a moment to find myself, but also to find silence in which I could actually listen.

I packed a bag, turned off my cell phone, turned off my voice, and ventured down California's great ocean highway, winding my way to a contemplative life among the monks.

I arrived later than expected to find a dark compound and no welcome desk.

Where else would you find monks but the chapel? There, in the dark silence, were three lit candles on a stone altar in the middle of the beautiful octagonal chapel with a small cross hanging from a twenty-foot cable. The candlelit marble floor provided enough light for me to see an assortment of monks in their off-white robes, along with a handful of outsiders like myself, on prayer cushions sitting against the walls. All attention was focused on silent meditation and reflection. No one seemed to know I was there, so I simply took an empty space on the floor against the wall as quietly as I could.

I wondered how much I would miss my family, what thoughts I would have running through my mind about work or the future, but they didn't come. This retreat, this moment in time where I allowed myself to let go, to truly let go, created enough space in the dark silence to let me connect my heart with my spiritual side. It allowed my cognitive thought process, the racing coconut between my ears, time to rest... and to not clutter up true peace.

Never have I enjoyed the dark and silence as much as that first evening. Although I was all alone with my thoughts, I felt cloaked like my neighboring monks, enveloped in love rather than fabric. Months later, I learned that a dear friend, one of my mentors, had passed away that same night. In retrospect, I believe his spirit was with me.

"DUKE"

harlie Shelton, S.J., had been my psych professor during my freshman year at Regis University in Denver, Colorado. I played baseball there before injuring my arm and transferring to Marquette University in Milwaukee the year my brother died. Charlie helped me through the difficult time with my injury, which had ended my sports career. As a clinical psychologist, professor, Jesuit priest, and friend, he offered much wise perspective over the years. He flew to Milwaukee to be with me the week after my brother died.

Charlie was also a committed Chicago Bears fan and we had a life-long, $1 bet on every Packer/Bear football game. This kept us in touch over the years during my journey and my search for meaning and purpose.

Nicknamed "Duke" because of his love of John Wayne, Charlie became a friend, although we rarely saw one another, who was always a phone call or email away. I wrote him the closest thing to a love letter I have ever written another man one week before leaving for the retreat in Big Sur.

I don't know why exactly, but I had come to a pivotal point in my marriage and asked "Duke" to keep my journey in his prayers. I also told him what his friendship meant to me throughout the years as I navigated life. I told him I loved him. It was the love for a friend who offered wisdom and unconditional love. I never received a response. Months later, when I tried to collect my $1 winnings from a Packer victory that fall, I learned Duke had died of a rare illness. Coincidentally, he passed away that first day of my retreat. Duke would have received my letter days before his untimely death. I don't believe in coincidences. I believe we are all connected in some strange, unexplained way.

Back to the retreat. I walked outside the chapel late that evening after hours of sitting in contemplative silence. The stars in Big Sur above my head made the Milwaukee museum's Imax Planetarium look out of focus and distant. It sure helps heighten your awareness of creation when you see the intricate beauty of the Universe just past your nose.

Some people find that transcendental moments make them feel tiny in the big picture. However, I found this one to be a gift just for me. Thankfully, I possessed the ability to appreciate beauty and poetry in an unending universe of which I felt an integral part. It put my life into perspective. I am not alone on this spinning rock among the stars; rather, I am sharing this creation with everyone under its shimmering light. And if I am sharing something, then I have a responsibility to help others appreciate all its beauty. This gave me purpose.

I went to bed that evening at peace and awoke to an even greater sense of purpose, one of newness. Daytime at the hermitage in Big Sur brought a whole new reality of the mountainous cliffs that spill into the sparkling ocean below. The morning haze of the Californian coastal fog made me feel like I was in a landscape watercolor painting. Then the birds and wildlife came alive. The views spoke to me in silent beauty.

There is a time for everything and this was my time. I can assure you that it had taken far too long to find this safe haven of peace, prayer, and reflection. I do not know of anyone who, after reflective downtime, regrets experiencing such a retreat into the depth of their hearts, but I know countless people, including myself, who on the front end, avoid the inner calling to relax, reflect, and reconnect with what is truly important in life.

To be the best father, the best companion, the best colleague, the best volunteer, the best teacher, or the best friend possible, I need to be in-tune with my spiritual self. There is such a sense in our culture of "putting your nose to the grindstone," "sucking it up," "toughing it out," and "getting over it," that we lose the core principle of humility. This humility—that I cannot do everything on my own—is a key to the healthy, spiritual, pivotal life. If you have this, you will have an inner awareness and confident peace about you that will emanate to all those around you.

Before things pile up too high, or you distance yourself too far from your relationship with the spiritual self, take a retreat somewhere small, or somewhere grand, where you can listen to the calling in your life. Make it a part of your yearly "tune-up" to keep you moving toward being the most authentic person you can be. Take mini-retreats during your week to sit in silent respect of all that you have been given; the air we breathe, the sun that gives life, nature that provides beauty, friendships that provide compassion and connection, family that provides security, hugs that provide comfort, work that provides purpose, touch that provides healing, and something bigger than yourself that cares and offers unconditional love.

The Pivotal Life necessitates taking a step back to look at where you are and where you have been, and then allows you the space to contemplate the continued journey. This is the part of your compass that provides a bearing relative to your current course.

> *A wise old owl sat on an oak,*
> *The more he saw, the less he spoke.*
> *The less he spoke, the more he heard.*
> *Why aren't we like that wise old bird?*
> —Charles M. Schultz

REFLECTION QUESTIONS

- When was the last time you truly took a break away from all your activities, duties, and stressors to reflect on where you have been, where you are at, and where you are heading?

- How can you set aside time to consistently reflect?

- If you find yourself off course, where will you turn for perspective?

NOTES

Shared Life

THE HUMAN CONNECTION

Love is all we have, the only way that each can help the other.
—Euripides

Although life's journeys are often taken alone, many also include someone cheering you on, empathizing, or admiring you from the shore. Every once in a while, it is good to look for that message of encouragement in the bottle that happens to wash up on the shore, or to even let someone on board and share his or her connection. You may be surprised about what you can learn about living the pivotal life from others. Sometimes it is much simpler than you would think.

As I cinched my tie in front of my bathroom mirror, I thought about my date night. It had been far too long since I put everything aside to embrace that which was most important to me. I had taken my eyes off one particular lighthouse in my life.

When she walked down the stairs of our home, I saw a transformed young woman, wrapped in a flowing shawl over a ruby-colored dress. Her hair was done and her blue eyes shimmered beneath her braids. She was a beautiful lady, eager to be my date to the symphony. I hadn't appreciated her quite like this before.

As all good dates go, I did my best to make her feel special. That was easy. It is so easy to take special people in life for granted, but this night, that would not happen.

I opened the car door for her and made sure her dress was tucked securely in before we set off.

When we arrived at the Marcus Center for the Performing Arts in downtown Milwaukee that February evening, we walked into the grand lobby filled with other special people on special dates. I gathered her coat, she re-wrapped her shawl, and we had something to drink while discussing the symphony. She had never been to one before. I could feel many eyes on us as we laughed and looked out the windows across the glittering downtown nightscape.

The overhead lights blinked, announcing the start of the concert. She took hold of my arm as we followed an usher to our seats right up front. This time I could see all the eyes on us as we moved into our seats. Smiles were plentiful and comments made on my date's pretty dress.

As the orchestra began, her eyes widened. The blended sounds caused her to smile almost with apprehension to the growing pace of the next instrument's arrival. She whispered an assortment of questions and innocently searched for what sound came from what instrument. She offered her best guess to me by pointing excitedly. I had chosen the right place, the right date for us. She loved it.

At one point during the concert, a few musical pieces in, I could feel her looking at me as I floated on the magnificent music. It was reconfirmed as I slowly looked over. She could tell I was also completely enthralled by the performance. She looked at me with the most caring and beautiful blue eyes, kissed my cheek, and said, "Daddy, I love you!"

My nine-year-old daughter Cecilia re-captured my heart at that moment, just as she had the first time I held her in my arms and she looked into my eyes in the delivery room.

With one graceful movement, she moved from her seat onto my lap, where we watched and listened to the remainder of the concert.

Cecilia was by far the youngest person at the concert that evening, and surely the only person on someone's lap. She was a single spring flower in the snow. I didn't care if our new seating arrangement was poor etiquette for a fancy symphony. I didn't have a care in the world at that moment except for the amazing bond between father and daughter. I felt unconditional love in that pivotal moment. It was a connection that I will cherish the rest of my life.

I learned that evening, surrounded by musical genius and appreciating eyes, that *The Pivotal Life* is one worth sharing. Shared love is a life force that will put wind in your sails. It certainly warmed my soul on a cold winter's night.

Although I might not always brush Cecilia's hair without tangle or pull, I know we have a permanent connection that works through the snags of life. The roots of our connection run deep, just as east needs west.

From the first day Cecilia and I connected in the delivery room, we worked together to communicate our love. I learned to understand her whimpers, coos, and cries and she saw in my eyes what brought me joy and even frustration. She felt protection and comfort in my arms, while I learned sensitivity and nurturing.

Over the years, the blue of her eyes has deepened and reminds me of the blue sea of possibilities. I yearn to give her the tools to navigate the vast sea of life, all while not wanting to let go, as I know I must someday. In my heart, knowing I have provided a compass for a loved one makes it a bit easier to eventually let go.

My daughter Cecilia and I on our annual date night to the symphony

Although I may not be the best father, I am her best "Daddy." No matter whether it's in a pretty dress and elegant hairstyle, or play-muddied jeans, she will always be my little lighthouse. She will forever give me purpose and guidance. She makes me want to see the world through her beautiful eyes.

The Pivotal Life must be viewed with the curious and innocent eyes of a child, where there is wonder and excitement. When life's symphony hits its highs and its lows, it is those with open hearts and minds who hear the calling. The ancient Sirens are beckoning. I am learning to witness life with curiosity to see how all its parts interact and blend together in a symphony.

During your journey, look to those people you can connect with. *Shared Life* is a pivotal point of the compass that will lead you to discovering purpose. Learn to appreciate and communicate with your network of friends, family, and mentors. Look inside each person you encounter for their unique gifts and talents. In turn, allow them to love you. As you do, the process of sharing will be life-giving. The connection will make you happier, safer, and more hopeful.

REFLECTION QUESTIONS

- Who is the "Cecilia" in your life? Someone to whom you are connected unconditionally?

- What people have supported you in the past who may only be a call or email or Facebook message away?

- What are some ways you can start connecting or re-connecting with friends and family?

NOTES

MOVEMENT

THE HOPE-FILLED SEARCH

Oft hope is born when all is forlorn.
—J.R.R. Tolkien, *The Return of the King*

According to a 2013 report published by the Centers for Disease Control (CDC), 29 percent of high school students self-reported they felt sad or hopeless almost every day.

Hopeless? Adolescence should be a time of exploration and discovery. It should be filled with happiness, wonder, and opportunity. It should be a time when young people are embraced with safety and love as they develop. There is plenty of time later in life to encounter hopelessness with mismatched careers, bills, broken relationships, and illness. If you cannot be "hopeful" during adolescence you are in for a long haul in life's journey.

This unfortunate statistic begs the questions, "Why do people feel 'hopeless' and how did they get there?" If there is a place that is diametrically opposed to living *The Pivotal Life*, it is a state of hopelessness. It is even more distant than living a complacent life. The complacent life is one of settling for the status quo. It means just "chugging along." Hopelessness is being stuck in a rut where there is little or no movement.

On the other hand, a pivotal life is one of opportunity and anticipation. It is filled with hope, which in turn is fuel for living, with constant motion, seeking and finding purpose.

It is draining to feel that that there is no purpose to life. Monotony, stagnation, and despair move in and begin to suck away your energy and confidence. Although I had moments of finding strength and rebirth following the death of my brother, and later discovered purpose in my work with youth and the poor, I had lost focus. I found myself sliding back into complacency. It wasn't hopelessness as much as it was frustration. I knew better.

Once you taste *The Pivotal Life*, the bar is set high and you yearn to recapture the feelings of drive, meaning, and direction. I was frustrated that the word "pivotal" no longer applied to my life.

THE MOVE BACKWARDS

After a number of years in various exciting, yet demanding, non-profit educational settings, including graduate school, I decided to throw my hat into the pharmaceutical world as a career. I needed a break before I burned out. The hours were more practically structured for starting a young family. My brother had been on the user end of pharmaceuticals; my sister and her husband were on the chemistry end, and Jennifer was on the sales end.

I felt I had an enthusiastic sales personality and loved meeting new people. Sales were right up my alley, or so I thought. The pharmaceutical arena may get some negative publicity due to the costs of medicines, but I respected my family in that industry and felt I could be ethical and earn a good living, while providing more stability for my growing family.

As fulfilling as non-profit work can be, it can also eat away at your time and pocket book. As the saying goes, "You don't know what you've got 'til it's gone." What I soon learned was that while the corporate sales world filled my pockets, it was also emptying my soul.

Within a few years, two pivotal moments occurred that made me want out of that industry. The first was when I was calling on a doctor in a free clinic. I was promoting a medicine for treating sexually transmitted diseases (STDs). In my carefully pressed suit, briefcase in hand, filled with the latest and greatest CDC data that supported my medicine and its benefits, I reviewed my information in the waiting room, preparing to give all the reasons why my medicine would cut down on the symptoms of an STD.

While I was waiting, a teenage girl entered the clinic and sat down next to me, also there to see the doctor. She was alone, shaking, and an emotional wreck. I can only guess what number of reasons brought her into the clinic. She went in to see the doctor before me.

What transpired over the next twenty minutes forever put my career vocation into perspective.

Although HIPAA privacy laws prevent medical professionals from discussing their patients, even to pharmaceutical representatives, they do share general cases with the reps to help determine the best course of treatment. The doctors, of course, had many more hours of training in the medical field than I. Nevertheless, I had a specific focus in one area of medicine that interested them.

Quality doctors like to know of any new data that could assist them in staying up-to-date on the latest and greatest. Due to the nature of sexually transmitted diseases, doctors seemed to want to process the unfortunate circumstances many of their patients were in. It must be hard to see patients all day long, five days a week, and not have many people in whom to confide.

This particular doctor told me about a patient she had just seen, not realizing that I was aware to whom she must be referring—the girl who had sat down next to me in the waiting room. The doctor confided that the teenager had gotten in over her head in a sexual encounter with an older boy, who had given her genital herpes. She had no one in her life as a trusted friend or adult with whom she could share this, and she felt all alone. She had no insurance because of a broken family and couldn't bring herself to tell anyone about her situation to get financial assistance.

The encounter put my career vocation into perspective. I was always happy to give samples of my medicines to those doctors who had patients in need. In that instance, however, it hit me like a ton of bricks that I was on the wrong end of the equation. I was only the Band-Aid, after the fact. The damage had been done. And there I was, benefiting financially from people who were in need!

My passion was helping young people make good decisions on the front end. It became so crystal clear to me at that moment that I wanted to help people like that teenage girl. I wanted to help them, either to not find themselves in this dire situation, or to help youth like the young girl find and develop trusted mentors in their lives, so that when the shit hits the fan, they have someone at their side.

Given her circumstances, the teenage girl most likely had a terrible and empty outlook on relationships that provide illness rather than respect. She now feels alone with no one to turn to. She now has a virus in her that will be with her for the rest of her life. She will have to start each future relationship on a negative note by sharing the fact that she has a contagious disease with painful and embarrassing outbreaks. All that and she hasn't even driven a car yet. Where is her hope?

Like the young woman, I also left the clinic that day with little hope and feeling helpless.

Fast-forward some months. My pharma job was about sales goals, rather than lives and relationships. Surely it wasn't about building up someone's self-esteem and self-awareness so that he or she could navigate life's obstacles.

It was the end of the sales quarter and additional funds had been allocated to our sales team. I received instructions to spend a surplus $4,000 by the end of the quarter, only weeks away. The frugal and logical side of me told management to put the funds back into research and development of new medicines. In no uncertain terms, I was told, "Use it or lose it." If we didn't expend the dollars we were given, our team would not be allocated more in the next quarter.

Big corporate America was rearing its illogical head to me. It was demanded that I spend those additional funds. The trouble was, I couldn't throw together any more speaker education programs in that short time. Most definitely, I could not squeeze in enough doctor lunches, during which physicians make time to listen to our sales pitch while they eat.

All I could do with those dollars was to buy "treats" for clinics and their medical staff and hope they would spend some time with me munching on a brownie while I updated them on my products. I simply could not do enough of these "Meet and Treats" to spend that kind of money. Doctors' offices often do not see sales reps outside of the scheduled appointments that are planned months in advance, unless the nurses smell sweets. Those calorie bombs were our calling cards.

I was so frustrated. All I could do was find a restaurant that made overpriced, chic-type cupcakes and bought 1,000 of them. I had become a caterer, a donut boy, spending money from hard-working citizens who bought expensive medicines and paid high premiums on their healthcare insurance.

By the last day of the quarter, I knew I wouldn't be able to unload all the cupcakes. I felt so pathetic that I turned into a homeless shelter parking lot that ran a meal program. I walked inside with over 500 designer cupcakes. I placed them on the counter next to the pans of creamed corn and mashed potatoes. I was asked who had donated the amazing treats and I simply said, "An anonymous friend," as I quickly took off my company nametag.

After that episode, I knew my days in pharmaceutical sales were numbered. As fate would have it, the three drugs in my portfolio—billion-dollar, irreplaceable products— went generic, meaning the trademark had expired and any firm could produce the drugs. That meant massive layoffs of the sales force. I gladly welcomed my severance package.

This gave me hope. I was freed up to dream about my future again and explore my purpose. Life is interesting. It continues to surprise me how quickly you can lose focus if you take your eyes off your calling for just a moment.

My purpose in life surely wasn't to hand out Band-Aids and cupcakes.

MY PIVOTAL SECRET

When my severance package ended, I was too proud to collect unemployment because I knew I could get a job somewhere. Financial assistance was most needed for those who truly could not find work, and those without a second income from a spouse. I wanted my next career move to be the right one. I wanted to be proud of who I was. I wanted my children and friends to see that I was being authentic and following my talents. I wanted meaning to shine from within. Once again, I needed to pull out my compass and summon the wisdom of someone I respected and trusted.

Michael Himes, S.J., a very wise professor at Boston College, where I went to graduate school, shared a secret to success. I remember him telling his students the following. "To better understand your vocational calling (what you were meant to do), you should ask yourself three questions:

1. What brings you joy?
2. What are you good at?
3. How does it make a difference in the world by helping someone else?"

Dr. Himes' teaching was that if those three things were operational in your vocation, "you would be living out your calling and find purpose in life."

I began looking around at my peers and people years ahead of me. Many of them had one or two of these operating principles in their daily lives, but rarely all three. Some enjoyed what they did and it filled their pockets and increased the size of their homes, but they weren't truly helping others. Others despised what they did but continued punching the time clock out of financial necessity. Some loved the money. Some needed the money for the lifestyle they had set up and needed to keep up with.

As a teen, I had a poster prominently displayed in my bedroom that portrayed a tropical beach setting with a gorgeous, bikini-clad woman, a Ferrari, and a mansion with a helicopter out front. It read, "I want it all, and I want it now!" I enjoyed those visions of grandeur, with me as the mansion owner, but now recognized how empty those desires were.

So desperately, I wanted to address the void in my life and fill it with purpose. I wanted to unleash the potential I felt from within. I was wracked with constant guilt that I should know better. I got caught up with complacency, living someone else's—or society's—vision of happiness and success.

Every pivotal moment of awareness seems to be preceded by a dry spell of complacency. Simply put, purposeless moments find themselves strung together on a strand of mediocrity. Finding your purpose is only a ticket to start the journey.

Some people get on the bus in the right direction, but fall asleep and don't experience the ride. Some get off the bus by being lured onto an easier, quicker path. They have little patience. Some allow themselves to be led by others, by false prophets, on a different path.

Everything we need for the journey of *The Pivotal Life* is contained within us.

What brings me joy?
What am I good at and where can I improve?
And how do these things make a difference in the world
for someone else's benefit?

If you can answer those three important questions, sleep well at night, and wake up in the morning excited about the possibilities of the coming day, then you are on your way to living *The Pivotal Life*—a life filled with purpose, passion, perspective, and selflessness. Living a pivotal life is an ongoing process, one of self-reflection and continuous recommitment.

Being human is about being in relationship with others. There is constant change, constant compromise, and constant re-evaluation. For example, examine the civil rights movement. Constant change, constant struggle, constant compromise, and constant re-evaluation that led to greater and greater respect and discovery. Only through this process can one uncover the dignity of those with whom we share this planet.

These thoughts coursed through my being. Examining my pivotal moments in life made me so in tune with the world around me that I wanted to immerse myself in a search for my continued purpose. I knew I could not wait. One step at a time in a search, even if you don't know what you are looking for, will lead you to a higher plane of consciousness and self-awareness.

Two things that always evade me are patience and fulfillment. I am very impatient. When you look at the world as an opportunity to leave your mark by helping others, you'll never be satisfied. There is simply too much to be done. Call it karma or whatever, but when you selflessly help someone, you get an intense feeling of confidence that you can do it again, perhaps at a higher degree.

When I serve others in a soup kitchen, for example, I cannot look at my own full plate again the same way. I ask myself, "How can I share more?" This feeling is not guilt, but rather a deep humility that to whom much is given, much is expected.

How can I be patient? When someone experiences cancer, he or she never looks at life the same way again. That person sees every moment as special, as fragile, and with gratitude. I believe those who experience death or an illness, like I did with my brother, see life as a gift to be unwrapped, appreciated, and shared.

I have heard far too many stories of those who go through life not happy. They sacrifice their happiness for some self-righteous act of penance. Often, I hear phrases like, "ball and chain," "working for the man," and other words conveying dissatisfaction. Throwing yourself in front of a bus to save a child may be chivalrous, but giving up on living out your calling is just plain dumb.

The Pivotal Call

A great childhood friend offered me a job as his new director of business development for an aviation brokerage firm, buying and selling business jets. Why not? It gave me something to do.

Movement.

That's what it's all about—being in motion. You never know what taking action will present to you right around the corner. The key is *movement*—so you can actually get around the corner. I might have been the first person in history to go from unemployed and gardening to flying in corporate jets. I wish I could say forward movement is the answer, but sometimes you need to take a major step sideways before moving forward.

One day, while unsuccessfully developing the aviation business for our company (during the greatest downturn in the aviation market since the Wright Brothers gave us flight), I received a pivotal phone call. The man on the other end of the line said, "I'm not calling you about my jet. Rather, I'd like to talk to you about my greatest asset, my eighth-grade son. He could use some perspective and I am looking for your advice."

Ha, I thought. *All eighth-grade boys could use some perspective.*

Because of my past experience working with students and service projects, this father had reached out to me. He shared with me that he had asked his son, "What brings you the most joy in a week?" His son couldn't answer, so he quickly changed the question to, "What most turns you off in a given week?"

His son found this question much easier to answer. He said, "Church youth group." This concerned the father. As a man of faith, he felt that he should help his son in his journey toward finding purpose, passion, and perspective. I commended him on his concern and assured him that it was pretty common for a young person not to know what truly inspires them. His son just wanted adventure.

The father believed that if his son could get some dirt under his fingernails by serving others, the "rest" (perspective, passion, and purpose) would take care of itself. I consulted with some of my former service contacts and similar results kept coming up. Eighth-grade students were either considered too young to engage in many existing service projects, or the opportunities were not *pivotal* enough. The father had wanted to inject inspiration into his son's life, and I envisioned a need for a "pivotal" experience.

I called the father back and said, "If you are sitting down, I have a crazy idea for you. I'll take your son to a garbage dump community in Kingston, Jamaica, to work with some of the poorest of the poor children in the world. If that doesn't work, I'll then take him down the road to an orphanage filled with cribs with one child more physically and cognitively disabled than the next. If that doesn't work, I'll take him further down the road to an orphanage filled with abandoned children with HIV-AIDS."

The father didn't hesitate and put me on the next flight to Kingston to research the opportunity. When I returned, I informed him, "The kids living in the dump still live in the dump. The kids living with disabilities in the orphanage still have disabilities. And the children with HIV still have HIV, or have died. Nothing changes in these marginalized, dusty, forgotten corners of the world."

Immediately, he signed his son up—against his son's will. I asked if it would be prudent for a 37-year-old man (myself) to put up a poster at the nearest grocery store stating that I was looking for ten more teenage boys to take to a third-world country?

After joking a bit on what our strategy would be, we pitched our plan at two small, informational meetings for area parents. Within a week, ten more sets of parents courageously signed up their kids to participate. We had tapped into a void that parents and teens were searching for. The seeds of what today is Pivotal Directions had been planted.

Reflecting back on my experience, I have come to the conclusion that *movement* was an asset that allowed me to press on. I could have thrown up my arms and surrendered to the fact that I was a replaceable part in the mechanism of corporate America. I could have settled for a life "Working for the Man," accomplishing someone else's goals and playing by rules I didn't believe in. I could have settled, but I stayed busy moving forward, searching for other opportunities that were in my wheelhouse of strengths. These include thousands of hours or working with students of all ages, personal development in areas of character and service. That is why the father originally reached out to me for his son.

Applying the wisdom of my graduate school professor and asking myself what brought me joy, what I was good at, and how it could make a difference in the world, I found myself back on track to discovering my purpose.

Life is riddled with events that cause us to lose hope and stop moving. We cannot avoid challenges or the sometimes debilitating nature of living. We must accept that storms can destroy, but that the human spirit can rebuild. Hope may be all that exists, but it is the sustainable fuel we need to move forward. Eventually, the fog lifts and new horizons await us.

Continually question where you are at in life and if your actions bring you joy and purpose. If you are unsettled, trust that your internal compass will point you in directions to seek further.

REFLECTION QUESTIONS

- Do you feel you have lost hope, your identity, or even stopped searching for your purpose?

- Can you remember a time you felt you had purpose or were truly needed for something?

- Have you ever felt that you are living someone else's dream? This may be a life in which you have a significant imbalance of time spent and energy devoted to someone else's goals. How could you reclaim balance?

- Name a couple of small things you could commit to that would bring you joy.

- Does the concept of "passion" seem foreign to you? Passion is lived, not wished. How might you know you feel passionate about something?

NOTES

NOTES

OPPORTUNITY

A Picture is Worth
a Thousand Miles

Opportunity is looking through a lens at life and taking the shot.
—Jeffrey Wenzler

Opportunity could be viewed as a set of circumstances that makes it possible to do something. *The Pivotal Life* requires us to look at life as an opportunity to put our mark on it. Each of us has a unique fingerprint. Life presents us with opportunities, chances, circumstances, situations, and people to engage in it, to touch it, and to leave our indelible imprint.

Landfills can be found in every nation in the world. There, everything unwanted, with no purpose, spoiled, or broken, goes to decay or dissolve out of sight. Beyond the developed world (what some refer to as "first-world" nations), the poorest of the poor survive off these landfills, where they search for food, for materials with which to build their homes, and for anything that would have value for trade or sale.

The smells are unbearable, the conditions, incomprehensible. The people who live in or on the dump might be considered less than human—unless, that is, you meet them. It is then that your perspective will change.

I had the privilege of stepping outside of my "first-world" suburban life of Happy Meals, air conditioning, street sweepers, bottled water, LCD and LED technology, into a world of recycled life.

The community is called Riverton City. It is a shanty town that lies along the edges of the Kingston, Jamaica, garbage dump. Some of the poorest people in the world have made Riverton City their home.

Hidden between cesspool trenches, heaps of scrap metal, and mounds of decaying trash as far as the eye can see, exists a resilient, tough, and persevering population. Don't mind the goats and pigs roaming past the rusting walls of shacks called homes—they provide milk and food. The residents of Riverton have learned to survive by using and re-using everything at their disposal.

My senses were heightened and my perspective expanded the first day I set foot into the garbage dump community. At first sight, I was awestruck, then filled with sympathy. After that, respect emerged. I was transformed. I had discovered this lost and forgotten world by fate and circumstance. That pivotal moment continues to define my outlook on life.

To pay for graduate school at Boston College, I worked for the university by leading groups of undergraduate students on cultural immersion trips to volunteer in Kingston, Jamaica. I have returned many times since graduation.

It was during one of the return trips of volunteering — tutoring and assisting with recreation and painting with the children of the dump community—that I was captivated by a photo I had taken of a nameless boy. He seemed to represent all the children who were hopeful of a brighter tomorrow, yet were not even aware of the junk around them weighing down their dreams. The boy's smile was enormous, but so was the desperate situation that filled in my camera lens behind him.

I promised myself that on my next trip, I would find the boy. I wanted to know his story. I wanted to share his photo with others to inspire future volunteers, perhaps

The pivotal smile that started it all

encouraging them to want to meet these beautiful souls who were struggling in such poverty. With the help of the Riverton school principal, Mr. Junior Rowe, who has over the years become a friend, we were able to track down the nameless boy's mother

One day, standing in the dark, narrow hallway of a one-room school, behind a rusty, iron security gate, was a petite Jamaican woman leaning timidly against a cinderblock wall. She had no idea why she had been summoned to the school to meet me.

I introduced myself, towering well over a foot and a half taller than she. I was the first American she had ever really talked with. I brought out my laptop and clicked on her son's tiny thumbnail photo. As it appeared in full screen, his yellow school uniform and shining white smile lit up her dark face.

The boy's mother, Ms. Jenni, gasped and grabbed her chest with her hand. The joy and pride that welled in her eyes replaced any anxiety she might have felt from my foreign presence. As she stood transfixed on her son's high-definition image, I gently asked if I could use her son's image to represent our work in her struggling community. A broken "Ya, Mon" came from her mouth and a similar smile matched to that of her son's, spread across her face.

We began to talk about the photograph and how I came to have it from a previous trip's visit to the schoolyard. Our conversation led us out onto the playground into the bright, hazy sunlight. As we talked, we walked. She was a busy mother trying to survive daily life in the landfill community. We walked away from the school and down the shantytown street as she went about her work.

I continued asking questions as Ms. Jenni poured out her hopes and dreams for her children in reply, as if no one had ever asked her. Her thoughts were equally filled with her struggles and despair, but she was not looking for sympathy. She was matter-of-fact with her reality and seemed to understand that her God was still close.

Her son entered my life through a camera lens but her heart entered mine through a trusting and brutally honest dialogue. Two people who couldn't have been more different came together in one shared moment. Jenni had no reason to be so open with me about things most families do not share. But I asked anyway. Maybe it was my sincerity and humility that permitted her to be so honest and welcoming. Maybe it was my honoring her that opened a door to her life story.

A turn here and a twist there, we navigated around corrugated metal corners. I hadn't been invited to her house, nor was I assuming that was where we were headed. In fact, I had never ventured so far away from my group before. I was now in the bowels of the recycled jungle. I thought she felt honored by the fact that someone cared enough to listen to her story.

When you honor someone with a deep sense of respect and gratitude, you often become humbled by their response. This reciprocity continues to nurture the relationship of trust we share to this day.

When we arrived at what seemed to be one rusty section of a corrugated metal wall that looked like all its neighbors, she slipped her hand through a crack to lift a make-shift handle on the inside that unhinged the metal enough to slip inside. This was the extent of her household's privacy and security from the outside world.

Inside the gate was a broken-down garbage truck and another for which they didn't have enough money for gas. Up against the small structure she called home to six people was her laundry area. There was an ancient, poorly wired washing machine that she said gave her an electric shock when she placed her hands inside to keep the clothes churning.

The laundry line strung across the tiny yard (if you could call it a yard) made the space look just a bit nicer with bright, clean clothing hanging in the humid, stagnant stench-filled air. The corrugated jungle of shacks sat on the edge of the landfill. Each time a breeze wafted by, it brought with it the smell of burning trash.

Inside the ten-foot-high metal walls was something very disturbing, yet quite extraordinary at the same time. A hard-working mother had more hope than even she believed she could have. Within these walls, she had a purpose—to manage a household of young, innocent lives for whom she cared so desperately.

I stepped over the irregular ground, riddled with stones and metal scraps, to follow Ms. Jenni's invitation to enter her abode. The realities of a place like Kingston, and even more so, the poorest section of the city, Riverton, didn't leave room for embarrassment of the living condition. It simply was life for Ms. Jenni and her family. There wasn't much to compare and contrast to in her reality. Everyone around her was as poor. She was as resilient as she was hopeful.

Her stories of faith in a God who had not abandoned her family were inspiring. How could I not think back to all the times in my daily life where I complained of how a part of my house needed updating, or how something wasn't working properly and needed fixing?

I tried not to judge. I was a guest, and she was a gracious host. As I sat at her kitchen table in a room that doubled as everything but bathroom and bedroom, I began not to care about my surroundings as much as the openness this stranger was offering me. The garbage dump outside her door, and its foul smell, faded away like the Caribbean sun. All that remained were two people sharing their stories.

One of many stories that struck me profoundly when Jenni sat at her little table was her passion to help other people. Never once did I hear her complain or ask why someone should help her family during the course of our first conversation, nor the hundreds to follow over the past years.

She pointed beyond the metal wall separating her property from a wooden structure next door that was in shambles. Ms. Jenni told me of her neighbor who was dying from AIDS. Everyone had shunned the woman. Only Jenni was there to care for her, to feed her, to check in on her, to bathe her, and to help her approach death with dignity. That story alone gave me insight into her heart as a woman of character.

I quickly, but tentatively, asked her before our surreal conversation ended if she would allow me to bring some of my students to her home to meet her and hear her life story. She humbly welcomed us deeper into her world.

Later that night, I told my boys that we had a unique opportunity to get an inside look into the home life and heart of Riverton. Beneath the rubble and junk lay hidden, dusty gems. We had an opportunity to not just serve, but to be served by way of accepting the human tale of one exceptional woman.

We decided to give her something in return even though she had not asked. We went grocery shopping for her family of six, filling an oversized canvas piece of luggage with canned goods, breads, bags of rice, fruits and vegetables, and treats. My students enjoyed participating in this gesture of kindness, even though they hadn't even met her. The anticipation of kindness in life is just as fulfilling as the act of giving itself.

The following day, Ms. Jenni met us again at the school to help guide us through the maze of rusty sheet metal walls.

Three of our suburban boys heaved the oversized, canvas duffle bag along as best they could and stumbled behind Ms. Jenni along the pothole-pocked, muddy path. They were focused on the mission of reaching her home and trying not to fall behind. They moved down the path like participants in a three-legged race. The canvas bag sagged from the weight of the canned foods protruding from the bottom. Every time the grip of one of the boys slipped, or they readjusted the extreme weight, it forced the others to falter.

One of their missteps caused them to step into a muddy puddle filled with God knows what. There is no sanitation in Riverton and the neighborhood literally lies on top of the old landfill. The glop from the puddle splattered up against their pale white legs and oozed into their pristine, white, suburban tennis shoes. What happened next was a true sign of character. Instead of blaming each other for the misstep, or complaining about the nastiness that was all over them, they pressed on to fulfill their humanitarian mission.

Once inside the compound, the boys' goal reached, Ms. Jenni knelt down to tend to the mess that dripped down their calves. She took off their shoes and washed their feet with bleach and water. Her gesture was almost biblical in its meaning—the master of the household humbly washing the servant's feet. I can only think of these boys going to bed at night months and years later in their comfortable suburban homes, thinking about the humility and grace offered them by this poor lady.

Behind the recycled front door, the boys began taking the contents from the duffle. As each item came out, Ms. Jenni's smile grew wider and her eyes welled with tears of joy. What I witnessed on the boys' faces was what I now refer to as humble pride. The stories that followed were as numerous as the cans of food.

Ms. Jenni's life story, which deepens with honesty each time she shares with our Pivotal Directions students, could fill a book on its own. The pages would be saturated with tears, but also tempered with hope and joy.

Visits to Riverton become an emotional roller-coaster for those students who return a second or third time. Her story is a mixture of mistakes made, tragedy, struggle, unbearable grief, humility, humor, and conviction, all coated in love.

At age sixteen, Ms. Jenni, like many Jamaican women, fell prey to the advances of older men, and she ended up with a child to raise on the streets of the city market. Mother and child shared a piece of cardboard to rest on; they washed at the public water fountain. Their life had no benefits of what we have come to take for granted. Ms. Jenni was a child raising a child, and the dump community would eventually become their home.

The dump is a place where dreams are covered in society's waste and hopes smolder with burning tires. Riverton's shoes are formed by calloused feet that have no Nike Swoosh to brag about. Tummies go unfed for days, and education is secondary to attitude and survival.

Ms. Jenni shared the reality of eating from a buffet of expired food fit only for a pig. The dump has a complex system that even I, after numerous visits, am just learning to understand. The residents know of everything coming into the landfill. They know what garbage trucks are coming from Uptown, which from grocery stores, and even which truck provides the pig feed of chicken scraps.

Pig farming is ubiquitous in Ms. Jenni's community. The food pigs eat is made from a slop scavenged from poultry factory floors. The leftover and cutaway, unimportant parts of the chicken become the meal for a pig and an occasional, unfortunate fare for Ms. Jenni's family. A broth can be made from the chicken parts that provides nutrition, if necessary. It is a fact of life living in poverty.

One gut-wrenching story Ms. Jenni shared with our students, with her own children at her feet on the floor, was when she told us what she did when there was no food. She had found an expired chicken that had been left to waste. She washed it with bleach water to clean it of bacteria. She cooked it for her kids but, when she served it, her daughter said, "Mummy, I can't eat this; it tastes awful!"

If hearing this story wasn't bad enough, hearing her mimic the disgusted voice of her daughter, with her daughter sitting in front of us, pierced my heart. What it must be like for a mother to have to resort to that level for her children, and then to share that grief in front of her child in the presence of strangers. Humility has no further bounds.

Because I struggle with living in the moment and enjoying what life has dealt me, I tend to look down the path a bit and see what the purpose is for something and what I am meant to do next. This is a blessing and a curse. There should be a good tension between these forces. I like the saying, "Yesterday is history, tomorrow is a mystery, but today is a gift, that is why they call it the 'present'." It is one thing to like a saying, but another to understand it and actually live it. I struggle with staying in the present.

I ask myself "What should I do with this gift, this knowledge of the human condition?" This outlook cannot be better portrayed than through one of my earlier visits to Ms. Jenni's home.

Ms. Jenni's 8-year-old son, Joshua, was present one day when I took a student group to hear her stories. Jenni and Joshua showed us around their simple home and tiny yard out back. Next to a heap of scrap metal Jenni had salvaged from the landfill to resell, was a small, hand-constructed drum set. It was made up of paint buckets as drums and an oscillating fan cover as the cymbal. Joshua sat down on a bucket and began drumming away with two rusty screwdrivers as his drumsticks.

I'm not much more than a music fan, but what I heard come from that untrained drummer boy was a pure gift from above. He not only was extremely talented, but also had a passion for each strike of the drum.

I immediately turned to one of my students, a classically trained jazz musician with the Milwaukee Youth Symphony Orchestra, and asked him what he thought. We determined that jazz comes from the soul and some people just "have it." Joshua had "it." I started thinking of all the ways I could help Josh with his gift and passion. I made Josh promise that if he was good to his mother and worked hard in school, our group would bring him a real drum set the following year. Both sides fulfilled their promises and Josh received his drum set.

Then one day, a year later, when Ms. Jenni was again speaking to a small group of my students, Josh's world changed through a simple stroke of fate on an iPhone. Josh was sitting on my lap listening to his mom pour out her soul to our students when I realized he didn't need to hear such dramatic stories. I pulled out my iPhone and let him play a game. He was very curious, and before long, he was walking around the room, showing his siblings the games. I hadn't even noticed he had left the room.

Later that night, I was in my room downloading all the pictures from the day when I came across a short video Josh had made of himself. He had figured out the video camera on the phone and had walked around the house shooting random footage. One selfie video he took was of him talking to the camera… to me.

Over the years, Ms. Jenni's family had given me the term of endearment of "Uncle Jeff." Paraphrasing Josh's words in the video, he said, "Thank you, Uncle Jeff, for all you do for our family, for my mother, and I hope to one day take care of you like you have for my family." He said so innocently, "I would like to come to your house someday, but I don't know about passports and visas and these things. God bless you, Uncle Jeff. "

I stared in silence at my little phone that had such great joy and unconditional love contained in its message. That precious moment was as pivotal a moment as any I had ever had. I cried in the darkness as I re-watched his video. I made a wish at that moment speaking to the screen in the dark of the night, "Someday, Josh, somehow, your dream will come true."

I never shared that story until this past winter. Dave and Ann Braaten, parents who had sent two of their children—Hayden and Hanna—on my servant leadership trips, had me over for dinner. They had heard of my recent divorce and were reaching out to me to check in. During the conversation, they asked me about my future and what dreams I had for my non-profit organization, Pivotal Directions.

Instead of telling them of some new expansion I was working on, my mind went back to that little drummer boy. I shared with them how my dream was to make Josh's dream come true. Before I knew it, I had a $4,000 donation

Ms. Jenni and her family with their new passports and visas

for plane tickets to fly the family to the United States with Dave saying, "Jeff, make it happen."

On August 4, 2014, I boarded a plane with an alumna student, Callie Donavan, to bring Josh and Ms. Jenni's family to our hometown after months of waiting for passports and visas. All the families whose lives had been touched by Ms. Jenni's openness and hospitality in her meager home pitched in to make a 10-day trip of a lifetime become reality. If that was not enough, my dream was even further fulfilled when Josh and his sister Jaday were asked to perform on a local TV show, *The Morning Blend.*

During the trip, Josh and his family were taken to a Bradford Beach along Lake Michigan. He quickly disappeared, as energetic and inquisitive kids tend to do. When his mother heard some music in the distance, she knew she could follow his drumbeats. Josh had jumped right in to perform with a band called the "Samba Unit" that was performing on the waterfront.

As it turned out, the director of the band worked for the Wisconsin Conservatory of Music, and before knowing anything about Josh, or where he came from, handed his card to the family who was chaperoning him that day, and offered him a music scholarship. Four days later, Josh, the self-taught drummer boy from an unnoticed, disregarded landfill community across the ocean, was drumming on American live television.

Callie, the teenage girl who had been on three service trips to the Riverton Dump, and who helped guide Josh's family through the airports, was standing next to me on the

Josh and "Uncle Jeff"

set of the TV show. We were talking about how surreal it was that Josh's dream and my dream were coming true right before our eyes. She said matter-of-factly, "Jeff, when your dreams come true, you have to dream up new ones."

What began with a photograph of a small child in a forgotten heap of trash would lead his family from their handmade house of recycled scraps to my hometown a thousand miles away. A camera can capture an image, but only the eyes behind the lens can capture the potential of that image. I invited the child's welcoming smile into the lens, and also welcomed the child into my life. His mother would welcome me into his family. His family would welcome my students into their reality, and my student volunteers would welcome them into their homes.

My Jamaican family—Ms. Jenni and her kids

Although Josh and his family eventually had to return to their difficult life in Jamaica, I believe a bridge was built between our lives and our worlds—we will forever be connected. I trust you will enjoy many updates about Josh and other kids like him through the Pivotal Directions website (www.pivotaldirections.org) in coming years.

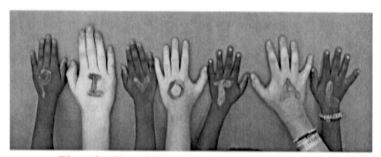

Photo by Pivotal Directions student, KK Doering

Opportunity awaits all around us. It is only through the gift of perception that we can conceive the potential of what can be. To live *The Pivotal Life* you must first be willing to look, and then capture the fleeting moments. It is in those pivotal moments that anything is possible.

REFLECTION QUESTIONS

- In what ways can you observe life going on around you to better discover opportunities for you to engage at a deeper level?

- How might you know when an opportunity arises for you to commit to engage?

- Opportunities come with successful and failed attempts. How can you best prepare yourself mentally for those times where a failed attempt at generosity might occur?

- List a few opportunities open to you right now.

NOTES

THE PIVOTAL LIFE COMPASS

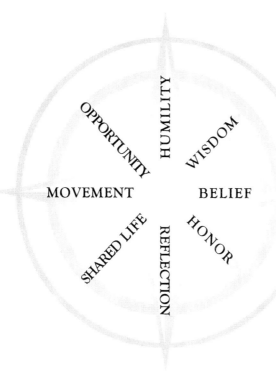

Each point a key component to living an extraordinary life.

AFTERWORD:
THE END IS JUST
THE BEGINNING

*What we call the beginning is often the end. And to make an end
is to make a beginning. The end is where we start from.*
—T.S. Elliot

Each of us has an internal compass that can help us navigate the journey of life. It can be a tool to help us understand where we are and how to get where we want to go. The compass is most useful when we are moved off course by the uncertain winds of life.

Life is a mosaic of experiences and relationships that beckon a response from our heart. It is these heartfelt moments (some good and some bad) that influence our mind and then motivate our actions. The "pivotal" moments in life are those that contain the ability to change our course. They have the power to move us in directions that may, at first, be unimaginable. These special moments may not always make sense, especially when they are staring us in the face, but we should still allow them to touch our hearts. Once this occurs, something much bigger takes over and pushes us forward with an even greater awareness.

This newfound perspective guides us further down our unique path.

Living *The Pivotal Life* is the pursuit of discovery. The more we allow in, the more we will grow. This will nourish us for the journey.

Although my own pivotal moment, the one that launched me on a fantastic journey to search for purpose and perspective, is unique to me, you too will have your pivotal moments when you start looking for them. Living *The Pivotal Life* is not about avoiding adversity, because you cannot do so. It is knowing adversity and challenges are coming, co-existing with difficulty and despair, and learning from them.

You do not have to look far for triumphant stories of strength and character in literature or film to find that ordinary people with extraordinary stories had journeys filled with humility. It is not even the *Rocky* moment of victory or the "Gold Medal" achievement that we relate to. Rather, it is that moment immediately after adversity hits where people crawl back onto their feet with a new perspective, motivation, and envision their success.

The following eight points of *The Pivotal Life* compass were gleaned from unique experiences I have had over the course of my journey discovering my purpose, passion, and perspective—I'm sure there will be many more moments along the way!

HUMILITY

POINT 1 OF THE COMPASS: HUMILITY

All too often, we hear of "the leap of faith," but what is that really? What makes someone want to leap with uncertainty? It takes courage to fall on your face, and even more to acknowledge a misstep. *The Pivotal Life* necessitates the courage to leap, and taking the leap itself. Yet it also requires the humility to fail and the acceptance of what that experience brings.

As your guide on this journey, I humbly encourage you to consider taking the courageous leap of faith into the experiences you have already had and ponder the lessons they contain. Once you learn how to look back at experiences you have had and reflect on what learning opportunities they granted, then you can begin to look at every encounter with life as an opportunity to grow.

The Pivotal Life is not a life of certainty and confidence; rather, it is a life of smallness and little control. The waves of life will take you where they will take you, but when you arrive, you will see with new eyes IF you allow yourself to accept wherever you are. Your compass helps you to know where you are at and how to get back on track.

WISDOM

POINT 2 OF THE COMPASS: WISDOM

Surrounding moments of adversity in life, there is a wise inner voice nurtured by parents, teachers, coaches, and mentors that we can access for discernment. Unfortunately, it is all too common for us to often avoid this voice for a variety of reasons. Those who seek *The Pivotal Life* learn to tap into the sage advice of those wise people who care for us, regardless of age, circumstances, geography, gender, or social status.

BELIEF

POINT 3 OF THE COMPASS: BELIEF

Belief is not hope. Instead, it is a deep conviction fueled by possibility. The story about the difficult pregnancy that led to my son's birth taught me about the fog of uncertainty that exists when we open ourselves up to love. Belief is the process of pushing forward even in light of risk. The second time I thought I had lost my son—while he was playing in the lake—I realized how fast the fog of uncertainty rolls back in.

Just when we think we have things figured out, we find ourselves humbled yet again, and dragged back into the mire. We control so little in life, but that does not mean we should love any less. The deepest purpose for living is for loving someone else.

HONOR

POINT 4 OF THE COMPASS: HONOR

To honor someone is to offer dignity for their life. To honor another human being is to endow that person with a deep sense of respect. In a world filled with misunderstanding, negative assumptions, and disrespect, honor is a gift that will lead you to a deeper appreciation of your neighbor. We must commit ourselves to honor not just those with achievements, or those who do something for us, but instead, truly honor the worthiness of every human being in our global neighborhood.

Although the disabled, aged Mr. Thomas at Mother Teresa's Home for the Dying was at death's doorstep, he taught me more than any educated professor adorned with degrees or titles. Honoring someone is an act of gratitude, declaring that he or she has shared a part of themselves with you. The mutual exchange between two people deepens our sense of appreciation and empathy for those different from us, those who reside outside our comfort zone.

REFLECTION

POINT 5 OF THE COMPASS: REFLECTION

Taking time to examine your life's journey and contemplating meaning in those experiences is the unique human gift of "perspective." Not utilizing such a gift is a missed opportunity. It is like being given a power saw and instead using an old handsaw, or avoiding a needed home repair altogether. Setting aside private time and space to reflect on our lives has major benefits. When we contemplate who we are, the moments that have affected us, the people in those moments who have formed us, our emotions and thought processes, our interactions with the world around us, and then take a deep breath, our perspective sharpens.

Everyone defines the "spiritual self" in different ways because it is unique to each individual. Reflecting upon your deepest desires, aspirations, disappointments, and successes, is a healthy way to become more self-aware and recognize your strengths and weaknesses. Understanding yourself and your place in the world provides great insight into where you want to go.

The Pivotal Life is not about time spent journeying or accumulating experiences. Growing in self-awareness is what makes us unique. It is what empowers us to live with greater passion and purpose.

Sometimes the silence of reflection speaks loudest and is our greatest teacher.

SHARED LIFE

POINT 6 OF THE COMPASS: SHARED LIFE

Almost every culture that has walked the face of this planet has subscribed to the notion that love is a gift that helps us grow in understanding and appreciation of others. It is a bond that unites us with others. Love allows us to respect others, to depend on others, to trust others, to honor others, and to protect others. If there was no other greater purpose in life than to love one another, we would aspire to greatness.

We need to be reminded from time to time that love is the answer to the greatest question of why we live and work in community with others. Discovering love, growing our love for someone else, allowing someone to love us, and not taking love for granted—all give us purpose. The trick is to participate in loving acts of generosity consistently and selflessly.

As with many of the different points on the compass, East depends on there being a West. Perspective must have a point of reference. Points on *The Pivotal Life* compass rely on each other. Love is dependent on Honor. Or is Honor dependent on Love? The first step to becoming more loving is to respect someone. Finding people to connect with on deep, purposeful levels allows for seeds of respect to grow and from that, great perspective and meaning blossom.

MOVEMENT

POINT 7 OF THE COMPASS: MOVEMENT

Hopelessness surrounds us. This is not to say that "the glass is half empty." Instead, the reality of sadness and complacency in our world comes in constant contact with us, and when it does, welcome those opportunities to push forward.

This pushing forward is what I refer to as "movement." With movement comes momentum. Whether we are the ones stuck in a rut with an unhealthy outlook, or whether we are directly affected by others who are spinning their wheels and sinking deeper, we have the ability within us to rise up and live a more pivotal life.

Often, this is easier said than done. The state of hopelessness, be it in a career, a relationship, or an overall outlook on the world, is debilitating. To navigate through this fog, we must access many points of *The Pivotal Life* compass.

To name just a few, we must activate the pivotal directions of "Honor" and "Wisdom" and "Reflection" of our internal compass to gain perspective. When we honor those around us and seek wisdom from others while reflecting on our current position, we will find clarity in where we are and where we want to go.

To gain perspective on where you would like to move toward in life, let me pose to you again those three pivotal questions asked by one of my college professors:

1. What brings you joy?

2. What are you good at?

3. And how does it benefit the world?

If those three answers are in harmony, you are moving in the direction of living *The Pivotal Life*.

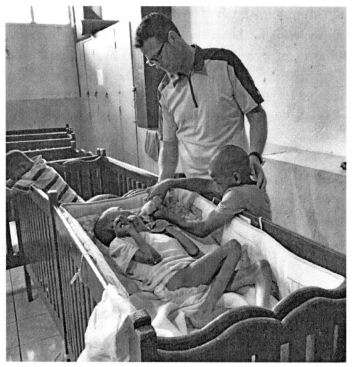

A special-needs child helping to feed a disabled child at Missionaries of the Poor, Kingston, Jamaica.

OPPORTUNITY

POINT 8 OF THE COMPASS: OPPORTUNITY

In the last story of *The Pivotal Life*, "A Picture is Worth a Thousand Miles," I utilized all the points and lessons of the compass to uncover an opportunity that would create even more purpose, passion, and perspective in my life. Although the story of the family from the garbage dump is unique to my journey, it highlights that opportunities for joy and personal growth can be uncovered in the most uncommon places if we only open our eyes.

If discovering a life filled with a deeper sense of purpose, passion, and perspective is a goal for you, then you need only look and act with courageous humility, seek wisdom from those who care about you, believe that anything is possible, honor all life, and reflect on your journey. Showcase acts of love and stay in motion even when times get tough.

This process is cyclical with great interaction like curling waves. Each point of the compass that helps you navigate the sea cannot survive on its own, just as you cannot discover new destinations only traveling West on one longitudinal bearing. As life sends waves your way, whether of great challenge or of life-giving force, *The Pivotal Life* compass will allow you to interpret, to discern, and to adjust accordingly.

The distant shores where purpose, passion, and perspective are abundant are much closer than you realize. Use your new compass with confidence to set sail on a journey into *The Pivotal Life.*

The End
is just the beginning….

Bailey, Cecilia, me, and Jonah

REFLECTION
EXERCISES

DO YOUR PIVOTAL LIFELINE EXERCISE HERE:

The Pivotal Lifeline Exercise

As freshmen in high school, my classmates and I were taken through an interesting exercise that has served me and many of my students well over the years. I encourage you to try it out.

Turn this book sideways and on the blank page opposite (p. 172), draw a horizontal line across the page. Place a dot on the left side of the line. This marks your birth. On the right side of the line, place the second dot. This represents today. The line represents your life journey. Along the line, in sequential order, place dots up until today where you have had pivotal moments. These could be a death of a friend or family member, a serious accident, a major obstacle, a victory, a defeat, a broken relationship, the birth of a wonderful relationship, a job, an anniversary, a memorable trip or a retreat, an illness.

If you need more room, use additional sheets of paper. If it helps, start with a brainstorm list at the top of the page or on a separate piece of paper, noting any event you can think of. Then hone the list down to pivotal, meaningful moments in your life.

This Pivotal Lifeline may take on your own unique approach. Oftentimes, during one of my retreats or work-shops, participants get creative with their lifelines, using colors. They will shade the difficult parts of their journey a dark color or make their lines synchronous with the ups and downs of their path. Some lines may begin to look more like trees with branches and offshoots of how the pivotal moments affected others.

Each of us will define "pivotal" moments in a different way. Some may think that they have lots of pivotal moments and others will struggle to find even a few. If you struggle to discover pivotal moments, start with pivotal people you have met. This exercise is about quality of reflection and less about quantity.

Once you have completed your Pivotal Lifeline, ask yourself the following questions:

LIFELINE REFLECTION QUESTIONS

- What was your experience with this Pivotal Lifeline exercise? Was it easy or difficult?

- Do you recall actions, reactions, or inactions during each pivotal moment?

- Are there more positive moments or negative moments?

- How might you respond differently to a certain pivotal moment if it happened again?

- Are you proud of your journey thus far?

- Are any of your pivotal moments unresolved?

- Is it possible to create a life experience that has opportunities for pivotal moments? (travel experiences, interesting people, volunteering, helping someone, stepping outside of your comfortable harbor)

DAY-BY-DAY REFLECTION EXERCISE

The ultimate value of life depends upon awareness and the power of contemplation, rather than upon mere survival.
—Aristotle

If there is any truth to this famous Greek philosopher's saying, it may bode well to explore how your daily life experiences shape who you are.

If you do not already have a journal, I recommend getting one especially for this new journey into *Your* Pivotal Life. Perhaps the Notes pages in this book helped you get started.

Take ten minutes at the end of each day to reflect. Find a consistent time that becomes automatic. Find a quiet and comfortable place without distractions. Sit with each of these questions for a couple of minutes and then move on. This exercise is not meant to be difficult, but rather to provoke daily thought about our place in the world and how we affect the world around us. Over time, these questions will become more beneficial than brushing your teeth. The three questions:

- What did I do well today?
- What am I not so proud of? Or where did I fall short?
- What will I do differently tomorrow?

SAGE EXERCISE

We are surrounded by elders, friends, mentors, and family members who can provide wisdom and insight on life matters and our decision-making process. Name at least one person in each category to whom you can look in the future for wisdom and perspective.

- Elder/Ancestor (living or passed): (Example: Grandma's advice. What would she have done?)
- Friend: (Example: Someone you respect, who has your best interests in mind)
- Mentor: (Example: coach, teacher, pastor, guru, rabbi...)
- Family: (Example: parent, sibling, relative)

What qualities and characteristics do each of these individuals possess that made you determine they are wise?

Elder / Ancestor:

Friend:

Mentor:

Family member:

THE PIVOTAL OBITUARY EXERCISE

This is a difficult exercise because it requires that you contemplate your departure from *The Pivotal Life*. If you could write your own life story in 100 words or less, in the form of an obituary, what would you want it to say? Humility has no place in this exercise. Step outside your comfort zone.

If you would prefer a different spin on this exercise: Write a concise engraving for your grave stone that you would like future generations to know about the life of the person who walked this earth. The purpose of this exercise is to have you reflect on the type of life you would want to be remembered for.

Life should NOT be a journey to the grave with the intention of arriving safely in a pretty and well preserved body, but rather to skid in broadside in a cloud of smoke, thoroughly used up, totally worn out, and proclaiming "Wow! What a ride!
– Hunter Thompson

NOTES

ACKNOWLEDGMENTS

This book would not have been possible without the support and encouragement of my parents, Joe and Ann, who continue to unconditionally love me along my journey.

For my sister, Lisa Savin, who served as my sounding board throughout the pivotal points of my life.

For my three greatest creations and pivotal moments bringing them into this world, my beautiful children: Cecilia, Jonah, and Bailey. Your spirit of joy and hope give me daily strength.

For my Firefly, who lit my path in the dark of the night.

For all those families and students who have welcomed me and Pivotal Directions into their life. I trust our partnership in making a difference in the world started with friendship and trust, and out of it we see the world and our place in it with new eyes.

For Kathi Dunn and Hobie Hobart, of Dunn and Associates Design, my cover designer, who captured the feel and essence of my work.

For Kira Henschel of HenschelHAUS Publishing, who guided me through this first-time process as a book coach and publisher. Thank you for challenging me and listening to countless stories in order to uncover the pivotal ones.

For Dr. John Duffy and Jim Higley for helping mentor me along the path as a new writer.

For the candid feedback in reviewing the advance reader copy of *The Pivotal Life:*—Kathy Blume, Elizabeth Braatz, Ashley Buchholz, John Duffy, Nan Gardetto, Jim Higley, George Hoff, Neil Willenson, and Carlene Ziegler. Your honesty and friendship in this tedious process of editing is so appreciated. I value all of your tremendous, collective professional background.

For Ryan Anderson, whose friendship, encouragement, and belief in my purpose got me through my doubts.

For the wonderful children and teachers of Monsignor Angelico Melotto in Santo Tomás, Milpas Altas, Guatemala, and St. Patrick's Foundation Riverton Meadows Mews Early Childhood Development Center in Kingston, Jamaica. You showed me that smiles don't come from what you have, but what you give. You are the richest people I will ever know.

If it were not for the Jesuits of Marquette University High School, Regis University, Marquette University, and Boston College, I would not have been stirred to seek out the most abandoned and forgotten areas of society to meet the most extraordinary people. In particular, thank you to my Jesuit mentor and friend, Frank Majka, who modeled how to put thoughts and emotions into words.

In memory of Charlie Shelton, SJ, whose endorsement did not come before his tremendous life was called home. Thank you for teaching me the art of gratitude, Duke.

ABOUT PIVOTAL DIRECTIONS

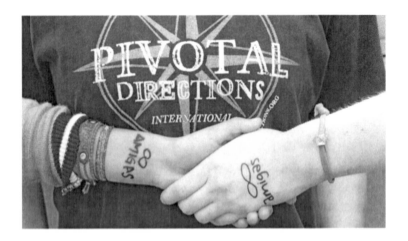

I n 2011, a dream became reality when it harnessed founder Jeff Wenzler's collective experience and passion to create a non-profit organization for teens and pre-teens to empower them with the spirit of serving others while developing character and leadership skills. Pivotal Directions, Inc. operates multiple global service and cultural immersion experiences in Kingston, Jamaica, and Antigua, Guatemala, for teenagers grades 8 to 12, including college peer leadership training.

Pivotal Directions, Inc. differentiates itself from other programs as an inclusive, non-faith-based organization by digging deeper, both in where we go and through our process of personal and team reflection. Pivotal also operates camps and workshops for youth in the Milwaukee area. Pivotal Directions has left its imprint on more than 5,000 lives—those of the participating students and those it has served since its inception.

WISH LIST FOR PIVOTAL DIRECTIONS:

- To tell the story of the hope, resilience, and human spirit of our friends living in a landfill community through a documentary film that can stir educational discussion about poverty.

- To raise scholarship funds that will help develop more globally aware, community-service-minded youth as tomorrow's leaders.

- To offer adults access to servant leadership experiences to assist in their development as globally aware community leaders, parents, teachers, and mentors.

Please visit www.pivotaldirections.org to support our vision or to become a part of the Pivotal Directions family.

THE PIVOTAL LIFE
IN ACTION:
"A DAY TO REMEMBER"

Writing a book is one of the most humbling projects I have ever pursued. I absolutely LOVE telling stories, and hope to grow old surrounded by those willing to listen while I breathe life into old tales and resurrect the meanings they may hold.

I believe to my core that life unfolds its petals ever so subtly, so that at times, if you are not paying attention, you might miss that amazing process. It is in the process of transformation that true beauty announces itself.

The following story, written by a former student, Ryan Anderson, is one I had almost forgotten. It humbles me beyond measure to share this story—I am grateful it is in my friend's words. It was originally published on the www.powerofhumans.com blog.

This is why I do what I do …

A DAY TO REMEMBER

This is the story of a woman who had nearly given up. And yet, despite her situation, she did not give up. This is a story about how doing the right thing and believing in your actions will lead to fulfillment. Further, this story reiterates my unfailing belief that absolutely everything in this life happens for a reason—a story of fate. This is the story of Faith and Ricky, and a white man with a special kind of heart.

Deep in the hills of Jamaica lies a dusty, forgotten road—a road that has been traveled endlessly and yet has not been repaired in decades. A mother and her son sit in the shade of a mango tree seeking a mere moment of relief from Jamaica's scorching heat. She looks down at her young, tired boy, Ricky, and sighs as she then looks up at the half-mile hike she and her son now face.

The hike was a daily ritual. To reach the rusted pipe that she used to fill her water jugs, she was forced to make the climb up the cliff-like ravine. To get food for her family and her animals, she was forced to make the climb. To go to work where she tirelessly cleaned a school for almost nothing in return, she was forced to make the climb. And to visit her husband in a dark, Jamaican prison cell, she was forced to make the climb.

Tired and hot from a long day of service in the Spanish Town orphanage, my good friend and I decided to take a walk. Along with my friend, I had been to Jamaica many times to serve the poor and have kept coming back because of the difference we are making for the locals. We walked down the dusty, forgotten road chatting about the trip thus far. We observed the uniqueness of the community...a man flew a brightly-colored kite too close to a power line; a soccer pitch with sticks bound by lashings for goals lie in the distance; and a group of goats ran by us kicking dust up in our faces. We walked on, admiring this land. Then, we came to a shady mango tree where my dear friend did what he always does; he started to talk.

Using a log for a chair, the timid Jamaican woman, whom we've come to know as Faith, responded cheerfully to the tall white man's questions. She gradually became more comfortable and eventually began to open up about the harsh realities of her situation. She had three children, no running water, and a prisoner for a husband. She was on her own trying to survive in this hot land and dealing with a life that mimicked the hill she climbed every day. She was losing hope.

I will never forget the experiences that followed, as they have changed the way I look at life, happiness, and faith.

As Faith continued to kindly answer our questions, my friend's mind began to turn. "How can we help this woman?" He did not have to utter those words; his body language spoke for him.

"Can we give you a ride up the hill?" he asked confidently.

"Well, I suppose so," Faith murmured uncertainly.

Excited by this new opportunity to serve another human being, the tall white man exclaimed, "Lead the way!"

Faith got up and ushered Ricky to follow her down the dusty path. We walked in a line through the bushes toward the road where our bus sat waiting. Saying little to the high school students on the trip with us, we boarded the bus and said we would be back shortly.

Not thirty feet down the road, my friend turned around with the look of excitement in his eyes. I remember thinking that he had another idea and then he asked the woman, "Can we buy you some groceries?"

A transgression of emotions flashed across her face...a look of confusion, fear, and hopefulness. She swallowed and said, "Well, I suppose so."

That was all we needed to hear and quickly we were en route to the grocery store. Farther and farther away from her hill, we drove across the bumpy, pothole-filled road. We eventually arrived on the smooth cement of the grocery store parking lot. The air-conditioned store provided immediate relief from the relentless heat. My friend and I each grabbed a cart and set off into the store. Faith with the tall white man and Ricky with me, we began to fill our carts.

It was apparent that Faith and Ricky were hesitant as we began to shop. Gradually, though, they started filling the carts with rice, cereal, beans, juice, milk, eggs, cheese, hot dogs, chicken, more chicken, cow livers, ox tail, and fruits of all shapes and sizes.

Ricky ran from aisle to aisle grabbing snacks—snacks that I later learned he had ever only dreamed of eating. His face lit up every time we nodded in approval and he was able to place a new item into the cart. These nods meant one less day of feeling hungry, weak, and depressed.

Faith had a different attitude.

She showed little emotion and simply pointed to things and said, "That would be nice." or "We could really use that." She didn't seem excited nor did she say thank you.

As the three grocery carts were filled to the brim and her attitude had not yet changed, my mind began to race. *How is our tiny nonprofit going to pay for this? Why is she showing such little emotion? Does she even need this food?* I wanted to check out and leave. However, my friend continued to nod his head as the two Jamaicans placed item after item in the carts. Even when we finally did get into line to pay, the tall American man had no problem with Faith running around the store grabbing more last-minute items.

My mind was racing. We don't know these people at all! How do we know they even need any of this food? What if our small organization was about to spend $400 on food for a wealthy family who took advantage of our generosity? We had no way to know for sure. All we could do is have faith.

As my friend calmly reached into his pocket and pulled out not the company card, but his personal credit card, the weight of the situation hit me with full force. My friend not only had more faith than I did, but he also put a burden on his own life simply to do the right thing for a total stranger. He said nothing, sought no approval, and didn't hesitate for a moment. This act reaffirms that he has a wonderfully special heart.

We pushed the carts out to the bus, where Faith and Ricky helped us load bag after bag onto the oversized vehicle. Faith sat in her center aisle seat with Ricky at her side, surrounded by mountains of groceries.

My friend sat in front of me in silence. I was still uneasy and unsure of how this whole situation was going to turn out. As my mind continued to race through the worst-case scenarios and question our actions, I almost didn't hear the tearful words being uttered right behind me.

Faith looked at the man who was no longer a stranger and started to repeat, "This will be a day to remember, this will be a day to remember, this will be a day to remember, this will be a day to remember."

A similar truth was born within my own heart in that very moment. As Faith realized the reality of her situation, I began to realize the reality of mine. It was through the selfless action and incredible faith of one man that a life had been changed forever and I got to witness it all.

As she became even more aware of what had just happened to her, gratitude poured out of her like a broken damn. In fact, she thanked us the whole way home. Her demeanor changed from apprehension to joy beyond all measures.

We then turned back onto the dirt road that was her reality. As we bounced up and down on our way up the hill, I could see in her eyes that the steepness of her life had suddenly become flatter. The road began to pave in her mind and become smooth. Just as the bus carried us up the hill to her house with ease, the selfless actions of one man lifted us up the hill of life to a house of better understanding and gratitude.

We stopped a few hundred yards away from her home and carried the groceries up the narrow, zigzagging path to her humble one-roomed space. I breathed heavily and rested not even a fourth of the way to the top. I then realized that this little Jamaican woman made the same hike every day ten or fifteen times. Not only that, but she had no vehicle to carry her up most of the way like we did.

When we finally entered the rusted metal fence that served as the boundary of her yard, we stopped for Faith to show us her water jugs. I lifted one of the muddy-water-filled jugs and realized in horror that it weighed more than all the groceries I was carrying combined. We continued up to her house, stopping at her 5x5-foot pigpen and the post that held her pet goat. We walked up the garbage-strewn path, avoiding broken glass and animal feces until we arrived at her door.

She showed us her home with more pride than I feel about the vast majority of my possessions. She pushed the door open to reveal a single room with two small beds, a dresser, and a nearly empty fridge. She opened the fridge to put some of the groceries away, and the only items inside were a fist-size bag of dough, a single onion, and a half-empty jug of water. Not even a meal for one. We asked curiously what she usually ate and got a simple reply…"what we can." We talked for a few more minutes and then she thanked us one more time as we began to make the journey down the dusty path. I hugged Faith goodbye and remembered thinking, "This will be a day to remember."

One can certainly argue that it was luck that was on our side that day. One could also even argue that what my friend did that day was risky and foolish. To that I say, everything happens for a reason. It was not chance that we chose to come to Jamaica, or that we decided to visit the orphanage on that day or go for a walk at the exact time that Faith and Ricky were returning home. We could have walked past them as they rested in the shade, but my friend and mentor chose not to ignore them, and befriend them instead. He chose to take the risk, step out of his comfort zone, put his own money on the line, and trust in God that all this was not chance.

In this world, there is fate and there are people who choose not to find the true meaning behind life's many so-called coincidences. I can say with assurance that any act of kindness, selflessness, or service to another human being will always lead down the path of fate and into the home of better understanding and gratitude. That is the meaning of a pivotal life and that is where we should all aspire to be.

Thank you to my closest friend and my most inspiring mentor, the tall, American white man who lent a hand to a family in need. Those of us who are blessed to know this man are forever thankful. And if you ever run into this tall white man with his endless passion and love for humanity, it will not be chance. It will be fate—that I can guarantee.

Ryan M. Anderson is a native of Cedarburg, WI. He is an entrepreneur, adventurer, photographer, Eagle Scout alumnus, Kohl's Cares National Scholarship recipient and University South Carolina Pre-med student. Ryan currently holds the Pivotal Directions and Starting Point Leadership Fellowship. He is the assistant director of Pivotal Directions Servant Leadership student service expeditions and Milwaukee-based leadership camp co-director. He is also the founder of the ReLearn Foundation, a community-based charity dedicated to improving global education through the collection and re-distribution of school supplies www.relearnfoundation.org. With a passion for helping anyone and everyone he meets. Ryan dreams of changing the world through service to others and hopes to inspire others to come along for the ride. He thinks big and is never afraid to get started tackling the problems of the world.

Ryan and I in the Blue Mountains of Jamaica.

Living *The Pivotal Life* empowers you with the opportunity to step outside of your comfort zone and discover ways to engage the world and its members in a mutually beneficial fellowship. When you enter into the landscape of relationship with others and no longer know *why* you assisted someone other than from a sense of "because it feels right," you are in harmony with our purpose. You are meant to reach out and connect with other members of the human family. I think Faith helped me more than I helped her. I felt I had purpose.

A month after meeting Faith, the phone rang. My bus driver in Jamaica, Paul Williams, had driven past Faith walking her typical long journey to work. He pulled over, said hi, gave her lunch money, and she asked if she could simply call me to say thank you. Knowing Paul was now paying kindness forward was all I needed to hear.

The world is a bit smaller and more meaningful when you reach out of your comfort zone. In fact, my comfort zone is now where I seek out more people like Faith.

Where can you step out of your comfort zone in your everyday life? Where is your Faith?

ABOUT THE AUTHOR

Jeffrey Wenzler is the founder and executive director of Pivotal Directions, Inc., a servant leadership non-profit organization focused on developing character and leadership through living a life of service.

Jeff received his undergraduate degree from Marquette University in Milwaukee, Wisconsin, and master's degree in education from Boston College. He has worked in the corporate world, academia, and non-profit industry.

When Jeff is not leading international service trips, he is a motivational speaker, panelist on Milwaukee NBC-affiliate programs *The Morning Blend* and *What's Hot* segment, as well as parenting columnist for the *Catholic Herald*. In addition, he is a contributing blogger for The Power of Humans at www.powerofhumans.com.

Jeff is a single father of three children running a zone defense and enjoying every minute of it… while they sleep.

Jeff is available for speaking engagements, workshops, and life coaching. For more details, please visit: www.ThePivotalLife.com

CPSIA information can be obtained
at www.ICGtesting.com
Printed in the USA
05n2029240516